Gotham City

WHAT'S NEW | WHAT'S ON | WHAT'S BEST

Dear Time Out readers,

You are holding the new Time Out Shortlist guide to Metropolis and Gotham City, which Turkish Airlines have produced in collaboration with Time Out, to mark the launch of our new routes to these famous cities.

The US market is a major focus for Turkish Airlines, and we are proud and delighted to add them to our list of other US destinations, from San Francisco to Miami.

Metropolis has surmounted recent difficulties and tragedy to regain its place amongst the East Coast's leading economic centers, with a booming downtown area and great investments.

Gotham City has also overcome its mixed reputation as a tourist destination over the years. It is now a perfectly family-friendly city to visit, with a thriving arts and leisure scene and a revitalised Amusement Mile scene.

As the airline that flies to more countries than any other, Turkish Airlines' slogan is "Widen Your World". Visiting these two neighbouring cities will definitely "widen your world", so we encourage you to book as soon as possible.

Enjoy this guidebook, and enjoy your trip!

Yours,

M. İlker Aycı
Chairman of the Board and the Executive Comittee

Contents

Time Out **Gotham City** Shortlist

EDITORIAL
Writer Daniel Wallace
Copy Editor Cath Phillips
Proofreader Claire Hills
Concept Turkish Airlines/CP+B

DESIGN
Art Editor Christie Webster
Group Commercial Senior Designer
  Jason Tansley
Maps Anthony Huggins

MARKETING
Circulation Magazine Heroes Ltd

ADVERTISING
International Creative Director
  Adam Harris
Managing Director St John Betteridge
Creative Solutions Jack Woodcock
Creative Solutions Project Manager
  Marta Kacprzyk

PRODUCTION
Production Controller
  Katie Mulhern-Bhudia

CONTRIBUTORS
This guide was researched and written by Daniel Wallace.

PHOTOGRAPHY
Pages 3 (top left, top right), 8 MPC; page 3 (bottom left)/page 53 Gallery Stock; page 3 (bottom right)/page 39 Galeries/Offset; page 4 Turkish Airlines; page 5 Evan Hutchings; page 10 Pio3/Shutterstock; page 13 Image Source/Getty Images; page 14 Blend Images/DreamPictures/Jensen Walker/Getty Images; page 15 James Baigrie/Getty Images; page 16 Lonely Planet/Getty Images; pages 17, 43 Yadid Levy/Offset; page 19 SinFactory Media/Getty Images; page 20 (top right) Nycretoucher/Getty Images; page 20 (bottom left) Michael Hanson/Getty Images; page 21 Dosfotos Dosfotos/Corbis; page 22 Space Images/Getty Images; pages 24, 26 Jongcheol Park/EyeEm/Getty Images; page 25 A Katz/Shutterstock; page 32 Gary718/Shutterstock; page 35 (top image) Miguel Sanz/Getty Images; page 35 (middle image) Eduard Kyslynskyy/Shutterstock; page 35 (bottom image) Paddy Photography/Getty Images; page 36 George Siede/Getty Images; page 37 RyanJLane/Getty Images; page 38 Massimo Borchi/Corbis; page 42 EschCollection/Getty Images; page 44 Fred Ward/Corbis; page 46 Photovideostock/Getty Images; page 49 Eric Nathan/Alamy; page 51 Radius Images/Offset; page 55 Creative Control/Alamy; page 57 Cultura RM Exclusive/Lost Horizon Images/Getty Images; page 58 Tangyan/Shutterstock; page 59 Sean Pavone/Shutterstock.

COVER
Warner Bros.

About **Time Out**

Founded in 1968 by Tony Elliott, Time Out has expanded from humble London beginnings (the original London Time Out magazine was a single fold-out sheet of A5 paper) into the leading resource for those wanting to know what's happening in the world's greatest cities. As well as our influential what's-on weeklies in London and New York, we publish nearly 30 other listings magazines in cities as varied as Beijing and Istanbul. The magazines established Time Out's trademark style: sharp writing, informed reviewing and bang up-to-date inside knowledge of every scene.

Time Out made the natural leap into travel guides in the 1980s with the City Guide series, which now extends to over 50 destinations around the world. Written and researched by expert local writers and generously illustrated with original photography, the full-size guides cover a larger area than our Shortlist guides (which are aimed at the short-break travel market). Many of these cities, and others, are now also covered on our website, www.timeout.com.

Throughout this rapid growth, the company has remained proudly independent. This independence extends to the editorial content of all our publications. No establishment has been featured because it has advertised, and no payment has influenced any of our reviews.

Gotham City Shortlist

The **Time Out Gotham City Shortlist** is one of a series of annual guides that draws on Time Out's background as a magazine publisher to keep you current with everything that's going on in town. As well as Gotham's key sights and the best of its eating, drinking, and leisure options, it gives a full calendar of annual events. It also includes features on the important news, trends, and openings, all compiled by a locally based writer. Whether you're visiting for the first time in your life or the first time this year, you'll find the *Time Out Gotham City Shortlist* contains all you need to know, in a portable and easy-to-use format.

The Gotham City chapters contain listings for Sights & Museums, Eating & Drinking, Shopping, Nightlife, and Arts & Leisure; the Don't Miss chapters at the front of the book round up these scenes city-wide. We also cover essentials such as transport information and hotels, and include a city map giving the basic layout.

We have noted price categories by using one to four dollar signs ($-$$$$), representing budget, moderate, expensive, and luxury. Major credit cards are accepted unless otherwise stated.

All our listings are double-checked, but places do sometimes close or change their hours or prices, so it's a good idea to call a venue before visiting. While every effort has been made to ensure accuracy, the publishers cannot accept responsibility for any errors that this guide may contain.

GOTHAM CITY

"THERE'S NEVER BEEN
A BETTER TIME TO VISIT
OUR GREAT CITY"

BRUCE WAYNE CEO

Don't Miss

Von Gruenwald Tower

WHAT'S BEST

Urban Highs

Gotham City, once a byword for crime and urban decay, has risen above its past to once again stand tall as an economic powerhouse of manufacturing, shipping, and financial trading. Centuries of industrial wealth have funded world-class examples of skyscrapers and venues for the performing arts.

Founded by a Norwegian mercenary, Gotham City is today one of the world's leading economic hubs and a center of history and the arts. The city's most noteworthy corporation is **Wayne Enterprises** (box p45), specializing in research and technology via Wayne Biotech, Wayne Aerospace, and Wayne Chemicals; and playing a vital role in everyday living through Wayne Shipping, Wayne Steel, and Wayne Foods. The company's charitable arm, the Wayne Foundation, has given the city a welcome new lease of life after decades of neglect and street crime.

Notorious crooks have included a number of costumed pseudo-celebrities, who have been opposed by a heroic figure with a similar taste for outlandish garb. That figure is, of course, **The Batman** (box p63), the vigilante who is said to scale rooftops and zoom down the streets at night in an armored car. The Batman is much more than an urban legend, but so far he has eluded the press and remains one of Gotham's intriguing enigmas.

City neighborhoods

Occupying a peninsula surrounded by the cold waters of the Atlantic, Gotham City is a vital seaport for the trafficking of cargo and the transport of passengers, as well as a bustling fishery. Bridges connect to the suburbs, and ferries lead to the nearby coastal city of Metropolis.

Old Gotham sits on the original site of Gotham's earliest permanent settlement, a trading center for fur trappers and, later, a military fort. Many of the buildings here, including **City Hall** (p33) and the **Orchard Hotel** (p57), have a trapped-in-time elegance that no other district can match. The **East End** is emerging from a 1970s crime wave that left it devoid of local businesses, with new housing projects and a can-do optimism from residents that has helped reverse decades of depopulation.

The city's **Financial District** houses the **Gotham City Stock Exchange** (p34), which is also home to the International Museum of Financial History (both are open to the public). Notable landmarks include the **Buford Building** and the **Von Gruenwald Tower**. On Gotham's west side, the tip of the city juts out into the ocean to form **Tricorner Yards**, named for the now-decommissioned Naval Yard established in the early 20th century and made famous as a launching point for sailors heading to the European theater in World War II.

Head further north to the **Upper West Side** to take in the lush expanse of **Robinson Park** (p35) and visit attractions such as the **Globe Theater** (p52) and the historic gas-lamp alleys of the Battergate neighborhood. **Midtown** is Gotham's most visited district, popular with both locals and tourists. Here, you'll find **Theater Row** (p53), the **Fashion District** (p44) and the dazzling storefronts of the **Diamond District** (p43).

The upper middle-class environs of **Gotham Heights** (p34) encircle a number of residential conveniences including shops specializing in

organic food, and gated dog parks. Further out, the enclave of **Little Odessa** is a source of cultural pride for Russian and eastern European families, expressed in an annual celebration that packs boisterous crowds into Volczek Square. **Chelsea** is home to Gotham State University and the humming collegiate shops of **Kingston Square** (p44).

Burnley Harbor (better known as **Little Bohemia**) deserves credit for incubating a daring underground arts scene that has made its presence felt across Gotham, from electronic dance music to 50-foot high urban murals. Bleeding-edge artists such as Neil Richards and the multimedia sensation known only as Kim have set up unofficial residencies in the area, with many artists following in the footsteps of Robert Therrien and building oversized sculptures of dining sets and typewriters.

The upscale residents of **Coventry** have kept their neighborhood free from industrial operations, and its tree-lined streets are home to quaint restaurants, as well as the **Gotham City Zoo** (p34). **Little Italy** on the **Upper East Side** is known for its delectable dining options and has historically been home to the city's crime families, including the Falcones, the Galantes, the Sabatinos, and the Maronis.

North Gotham also contains the expansive blocks of **Park Row** (p35), which still bears the elegant hallmarks of its 1920s high period, which fell into disrepair during the 'Crime Alley' era that followed the murders of the Waynes. The adjacent **Bowery** fared better, and is a lively area of bars, nightclubs, and slightly louche alleyways. Gotham jazz got its start in **Burnley** in the 1930s, but today this is an industrial area home to petrochemical behemoths such as Ace Chemicals and Bryant Chemical Works.

DON'T MISS

Kane Art Museum p34

Amusement Mile (p32) encompasses the boardwalk along the north Gotham waterway, as well as the Newton Fairgrounds and Amusement Park. After a decade of neglect, the area is once more open for business, thrilling tourists with its revamped death-defying rides. The twisted antics of mad court jesters find their expression on this stretch. Bohemian artists have embraced the area's dark carnival reputation to indulge in experimental theater and retro burlesque. The **Gotham City Yacht Club** isn't far from here, though non-members will find only a high fence and stern-faced security guards.

Gotham's suburban communities include **Bristol** and **Somerset**, with the latter housing the infamous **Arkham Asylum** (p33) as well as the unspoiled acreage of **Slaughter Swamp State Park**.

Museum marvels

The city's museums are second to none. Highlights include the **Gotham City Museum of Antiquities** (p34), which showcases the treasures of antiquity and the splendors of long-dead kings; and the nearby **Gotham City Museum of Natural History** (p34), which has vast holdings in the sciences of entomology, anthropology, zoology, mineralogy, and paleontology. The **Kane Art Museum** (p34) is a provocative showcase for multimedia works and oft-neglected icons of popular culture, while the **Father Knickenbocker Wax Museum** (p33) is a ghoulish but fascinating collection of wax-casted stiffs.

Pinnacles of power

Gotham City is famous across the world for its imposing and

DON'T MISS

Gotham Heights p34

distinctive skyscrapers. Both **Wayne Tower** (p36) and the **Clocktower** (p33) can be viewed in one go if you get off the El Train at the Wayne Tower Station. You'll have to snap pictures of Wayne Tower from the street, though, as it's closed to the public. The chimes of the Clocktower can be heard throughout downtown Gotham, a regular reminder of the Wayne Foundation's generosity in restoring the city's neglected grandeur. In the Diamond District, the **Ellsworth Building** (p33) is an art deco masterpiece that's often reproduced on keychains and inside collectible snow globes. The clean lines of the **Davenport Tower** hide a popular shopping mall inside, the **Davenport Center** (p43).

Danse macabre

Gotham is a place of sinister smiles. True connoisseurs of crime visit up the **Arkham Asylum** (p33), the notorious sanatorium rumored to have treated Killer Croc, Siphnot, The Joker and other criminals. Gawkers frequently line up outside the gates, despite the city's discouragement of the practice. The island stronghold of **Blackgate Penitentiary** (p33) can be viewed

from Gotham's Lower East Side. Boat and helicopter tours give it a wide berth, which is probably a good thing given the frequency of breakouts from Blackgate's inmates.

Green and pleasant

Robinson Park (p35) has been a natural oasis in Gotham City for more than 200 years. Depending on the season, the Robinson Park Reservoir is the spot of choice for pleasure boating or family ice skating. The park's expansive west lawn draws crowds who fan out to visit the Forum of the Twelve Caesars, Giella Gardens, or the historical quirk that is Finger Castle. **Tricorner Park** (p36) is perfect for brisk walks at sunrise and sunset, and its promenade is crowded with joggers, dog-walkers, and guitar-strumming street performers angling for tips.

In **Neo-Eden** (p35), you'll find floral exoticism with a frisson of danger thanks to glass-covered exhibits of toxic spores and carnivorous plants. There's also the **Wayne Botanical Garden** (p36), a cozy and colorful escape from the sometimes dreary Gotham climate.

GOTHAM
IS SERVED

ENTITLES YOU TO **50% OFF** THE FOLLOWING RESTAURANTS:

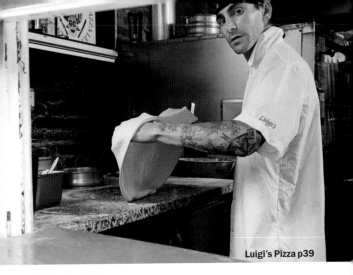

Luigi's Pizza p39

WHAT'S BEST
Now You're Cooking!

No single word can define the taste of Gotham City, where the eateries are as varied as the melting-pot of immigrants who have arrived in this welcoming port city over the centuries. Gotham certainly goes gaga for its restaurants, and if you want to sample its ethnic diversity and rich heritage, there's no better way than to dine at a different venue each night. Hopping between the city's many disparate and colorful neighborhoods will result in a mouth-watering selection of restaurants, each offering dishes that tantalize the tongue.

You could, for example, enjoy grilled orange pheasant as you watch the darkening waters of the harbor, then tuck into a warm egg-white quiche come daybreak. The boundless Atlantic Ocean has long made Gotham a seafood destination, and tasty fish dishes can be found on every street from the Port Adams docks and beyond. Prices vary hugely too, from budget noodle bars to haute cuisine hotel treats, with plenty in between.

Cheap and cheerful

You'll come across numerous eateries claiming to serve Gotham's best burger or best slice of pizza. **Luigi's Pizza** (p39) makes no such boast, but its generous pies appeal to large groups with varied tastes, thanks to an endless array of toppings and many options for vegans and those with gluten sensitivities. A stop at **Big Belly Burger** (p37) might not seem very adventurous, but over the years Gothamites have claimed the national chain as their own, resulting

Chinatown p38

in a custom menu with special sandwiches named after famous landmarks and infamous criminals.

Gourmet noodle bars have begun spreading far beyond their roots in Chinatown, and Tokyo-style ramen is now an addiction for Gotham State University students making their way back to campus from the late-night bars in Kingston Square. Elsewhere, the **Davenport Center** (p43) sits atop a subterranean food court tightly packed with quick and cheap eats – the place becomes a shoulder-to-shoulder crush on weekdays from 11am to 1pm.

Faraway flavors

Gotham's immigrant experience has produced some truly standout examples of ethnic cuisines, from Turkish grills to Chinese noodles. **Falcone's** (p39) has enjoyed an unbroken line of multi-generational Italian ownership and carries an air

of notoriety due to its whispered ties to a powerful mafia don. **Ciao Bella** (p38) is a rising star in Little Italy, known for a Venetian-themed menu that emphasizes seafood choices. **Finger Foods** (p39), near the Theater District, is Gotham's leading tapas bar, attracting most of its business from pre-show theatregoers in the mood for drinks and dinner.

In Chinatown, the **Red Lotus** (p41) offers five levels with distinct Thai, Chinese, Japanese, Korean, and Vietnamese menus; and many other oriental favorites line the walkways beyond the arch at Storrow and Foote Streets. In Little Odessa, tiny shops proffer filling Slavic dishes.

Elegant environs

Gastronomes can find plenty to please their palate in any Gotham neighborhood. In Midtown, **Fox Gardens** (p39) offer a relaxing lounge atmosphere amid the playful

Eating & Drinking

tones of piano jazz. A short but spectacular menu is available to a limited number of customers before the restaurant caps attendance, making dinner at Fox a bucket-list achievement for many. Over at the **Bristol Country Club** (p38), the chef serves up steak and lobster to formally dressed patrons in a style of cuisine that's gone unchanged since World War II. The **Blue Heron** (p37) in Coventry is arguably Gotham's finest five-star restaurant, with a 1920s cachet and an adventurous menu featuring dishes from every corner of the globe.

Rise and shine

A long day of exploring the city deserves a fully fuelled head start. After rubbing the sleep out of your eyes, head over to South Gotham for some of the best breakfast eats at the aptly named **MM Good Donuts** (p41). Skip the glazed pastries and enjoy the retro diner's real specialty by wolfing down a gut-filling chorizo burrito.

You can find a **Jitters** (p39) coffeehouse seemingly on every corner. More Gothamites buy their java here than from any national chain, and its red and brown paper cups are ubiquitous talismans in the hands of sleepy morning commuters. **Pamela's Café** (p41) is another hopping breakfast spot, and its long lines have become impromptu venues for locals to network and socialize while enjoying bottomless free coffee.

Happy hours

Tasty morsels served alongside buzzworthy cocktails is the latest drinking trend in Gotham. Based on the new venues opening in the Lower West Side and the upper environs of Midtown, the trend is primed to become a full-on craze. Young

restaurateurs have also spearheaded a new cluster of martini bars in the Bowery and a second one on the outskirts of Park Row, exhibiting a gritty sensibility that contrasts with their inspirations – the old-school bars adjacent to the trad steakhouses in Old Gotham.

The nationwide craft beer boom hasn't excluded Gotham either; lagers, stouts and ales bottled by local microbreweries are common on drinks lists and are frequently worth a taste. The **Tap Room** (p41) is a huge place, and with good reason: it contains an entire brewery and a smoky lineup of BBQ grills, all sitting atop a subterranean beer and wine cellar.

At the historic **Riverside Lounge** (p41), you can tip back a classic cocktail while feeling like a bootlegger; locals love the place. Over at the **Paradise Club** (p41), the sweet strains of New Orleans-style jazz are the perfect complement to the spicy Cajun cuisine and impressive whiskey list.

Falcone's p39

Fashion District p44

WHAT'S BEST

Curiosity Shops

Gotham City is vintage to the core. No other city seems to revel so much in its history and heritage. Its shops offer up both period clothing and retro-inspired modern looks by hip urban designers. The **Fashion District** (p44) should be the first stop for any true clothes-horse, with boutiques showcasing imported dresses from Paris and Milan alongside charming patchwork overcoats tailored to your measurements in under an hour. Just a short hop from the Fashion District is the **Diamond District** (p43), a must-see source of precious metals and priceless stones brought together in intricate and exquisite rings, necklaces, earrings, and brooches. There's plenty of shopping at the university hangout **Kingston Square** (p44), but you might get just as much enjoyment by setting

your bags down and relaxing at an outdoor café. Once you've recaffeinated, Kingston Square is the perfect spot for scoping out college and pro sports memorabilia – especially emblazoned with the logo of the Gotham State University Wildcats. Over in the **Electronics Sector** (p43), tech treasures can be found amid heaps of flashing and beeping imports of undetermined purpose.

The city's museums are unexpectedly rewarding places to browse for souvenirs and artworks. The gift shop in the **Gotham City Museum of Antiquities** (p34) sells replicas of the treasures of Egypt, and notebooks and fountain pens stamped with cuneiform characters. The Gotham City **Museum of Natural History** (p34) is the definitive dinosaur shop

Shopping

for the dino-loving kid on your list, and also offers rare fossils and mineral specimens at the high end of the price range. At the **Kane Art Museum** (p34), art for sale includes animation cels, movie storyboards, vinyl sculptures, and limited-edition signed prints.

Retro oddities

Quirky stores are a hallmark of Gotham, somehow subsisting on the few genuine sales that trickle in amid the parade of curious onlookers. **1 O/6** (p42) has been in business since 1919 and its bonnets, boaters, and bowlers are the perfect toppers to your convincingly retro ensembles. A similar experience awaits at **Alice's Antiques** (p43), where an imaginative re-creation of a 19th-century general goods store casts a convincing spell, right down to the pleasantly musty air.

In the narrowly packed pedestrian streets of Old Gotham, similar stores await your discovery. Seldom advertised – sometimes not even with a sign above the door – these places are hard to find and often, frustratingly, even harder to locate a second time, leading to urban legends about mystical vanishings. Expect to encounter freak-show oddities preserved in formaldehyde bottles, moths and beetles carefully pinned inside painted gift boxes, and masks molded from life-casts of convicted criminals.

Get sale-savvy

Trendy tastemakers too rich for your pocketbook? Don't worry: downtown Gotham and the city's outlying suburbs are home to outlet stores and discount malls (p44). **Davenport Center** (p43) and **Midtown Mall** (p44) are two notable destinations inside Gotham, while **Castleland Mall, Richland Mall,**

Davenport Center p43

and the **Crystal Palace** are reachable on the other side of the bridges via a short car ride. Post-season sales usually start just after Christmas and last through mid-January, with a second sales season hitting in June and carrying through the Fourth of July holiday weekend. Many stores in the Fashion District offer discount racks and sale tables to attract crowds of rummagers looking for a real steal. Check out the flyers in the *Gotham Freepress* for late-breaking bargains.

Flea markets pop up in the Bowery along Anastasia Street every Sunday from 8am to noon, and in Park Row along Barton Street on Saturdays from 7am to 11am. Such markets are ideal for discovering used clothing and jewelry, vintage electronics, handmade outsider artworks, and gloriously tacky bric-a-brac, and have attracted a devoted following among Gotham State U students and urban twentysomethings.

" Gotham jazz is back with a bang!
A must-hear musical extravaganza "
GOTHAM FREE PRESS

58th Annual
GOTHAM CITY
JAZZ
July 2016 20-25 **FESTIVAL**
Tickets available now.
www.gothamarts.got

Peregrinator's Club p48

WHAT'S BEST
Night Moves

There's something for everyone in Gotham City after dark. Gentlemen's clubs and speakeasies are retro fixtures throughout Lower Gotham. Dance clubs light up the night on the Lower West Side and the Bowery. In the Warehouse District and Little Bohemia, dimly lit loft spaces invite guests to partake in artistic experiments that have to be experienced to be believed.

Gotham's casinos are relatively new additions. The gaming action runs 24 hours, but live music and comedy acts are booked for evening showings. **Gotham City Olympus** (p47) is the high-end gambling palace, styled after Monte Carlo attractions and offering a similar mix of baccarat and roulette for deep-pocketed players only. Those with fewer resources to risk on games of chance may have a better

time at **Maxie's Casino** (p48), a smaller and noisier attraction but one with constant distractions with complimentary drinks and snacks. In the Diamond District, **Harry's Revue** is one of Gotham's oldest comedy clubs. Open-mic nights at Harry's are raucous and ribald, with audience members frequently turned into participants as the emcee tries to corral the improv energy.

Tastefully refined

Gotham has always had a moneyed upper class. From the Waynes to the Powers, families have held the reins of industry and passed down their wealth and power to subsequent generations. Nightclubs catering to the rich (and those who want to act rich) are numerous throughout Lower Gotham. One of the leaders is clearly the **Iceberg Lounge** (p47), unmissably positioned at the edge of the waterfront. This two-story restaurant and lounge operated by Gotham eccentric Oswald Cobblepot has an idiosyncratic focus on birds and umbrellas in its decor, with an exclusive VIP area upstairs. Former mobster Johnny Sabatino is behind **Club Vesuvius** (p47), with a retro 1940s look and a performance stage for musicians and magic acts. Along Lower Gotham's Electric Street, you can feel the hum of the current coming from exclusive clubs such as **Paora** and **Paz Rudi**, where the size of the bouncer guarding the door is a good guide for estimating how difficult it will be to get inside. Expect to drop some cash if you want to fully enjoy the **Tobacconists Club** (p48) – complete with mahogany paneling, crystalline chandeliers, and the ever-present haze of cigar smoke. The **Peregrinator's Club** (p48) is cut from the same cloth, but wears a deco-styled look inspired by the lairs of explorers and big-game hunters. Authentically retro, the place has remained largely unchanged since opening in 1932.

The **Egyptian** (p47) is much newer but still feels like it belongs to another era. Golden statues of

Tobacconists Club p48

the cat goddess Bast flank the front door and smaller versions can be found throughout the venue, along with hieroglyphic murals and themed tables honoring Horus, Anubis, Sobek and other deities from antiquity.

Music meisters

Live music is plentiful in Gotham. Nearly every genre you can imagine already has a dedicated venue, or at least a theme night that attracts legions of enthusiasts. From the-wall dives to the majesty of the opera house, venues run the gamut from seedy to sophisticated, with cover prices to match.

The famous **Jazzland** in Burnley has hosted great jazz artists since the 1920s and is the birthplace of Gotham-style swing. Rock and pop megastars fill sports palaces such as **Midtown Arena**. For indie rock you can't go wrong with **Gramercy Loft** (p47), a former warehouse popular with GSU students and a frequent stop for many national touring acts looking to play a more intimate venue. If you don't like what's on the bill at Gramercy, the nearby expanse of **Kingston Square** (p44) offers up plenty of alternatives. Taverns, coffeehouses, and cozy concert halls are busy from Wednesday through Saturday nights, but see light attendance during GSU spring and summer breaks. Amateur-night showcases

Gramercy Loft p47

Kremlin Club p48

and poetry readings are common on
Monday and Tuesday evenings.

Wild sides

If you know where to look, Gotham's
nightlife carries an air of danger –
and some venues proudly dip into a
well of lovingly managed insanity.
Underground raves can be found
throughout the Bowery. One of the
oldest venues is **KranKzz**, built
inside an empty chemical tank where
the dance music echoes deafeningly
off the rusted metal walls.
Electronica fans who care more
about sound quality than spectacle
should make a beeline for **27 Tek**
(p46), a club that employs audio
engineers to tweak the acoustics for
maximum fidelity. **Up All Night** is
a hotspot for experimental music if
you're hitting up the Lower East Side.
A hop over to Little Odessa brings
you to the **Kremlin Club** (p48), an
ironic tribute to Cold War Soviet
surveillance that spreads outlandish
rumours about its role in mind control
and the spread of undercover sleeper

Nightlife

agents. When it comes to a place like
Sions Below (p48), the rumours
just might be true – this notorious
venue is reportedly the site of a
backroom, no-holds-barred fight
club, but the venue's location
changes so frequently it has escaped
attention from the GCPD. The
Ventriloquist Club (p49) offer's
a grab-bag of entertainment from
interpretive dance to vaudeville,
with its devoted attendees never
clear what kind of show they'll get
on any given night.

In the unsettling fringes of
Amusement Mile is **Circo Roma**
(p47), a circus-themed club with a
freak-show decor. Its music is a head-
trip melange of calliope pipes and
thumping bass beats. **Amusement
Mile Burlesque** (p46) is proud to
occupy the skeletons of rotting
buildings, using the atmosphere of
decay and danger to stage playful
dance shows with stylish flair. In
the Bowery, the **Victorian Parlor**
(p49) is a recent addition to the trend,
recreating the velvety decadence of
a 19th-century neo-gothic den.

Gotham City Opera House p52

WHAT'S BEST

Artistic License

According to many Gothamites, the quality of their cultural scene is what elevates their hometown above similarly sized rivals – particularly Metropolis. While that specific claim is subjective, there's no denying that Gotham has impeccable bona fides when it comes to presenting and encouraging the arts. Twin theater districts – the famous crossroads in Midtown and a second burgeoning area in the heart of Park Row – regularly fill seats for ballet performances, classical concerts, toe-tapping musicals, and serious dramatic works. An underground arts scene hums just beneath the surface, supplying Gotham's more established venues with fresh talent and new ideas; Little Bohemia is the place to catch these experimental tastemakers before they hit it big.

Clowning around

Gotham City has a reputation for embracing and updating an old-fashioned vibe, one that's tinged with faded melancholy. Nowhere is that more evident than **Amusement Mile** (p32). This busy boardwalk attraction is proud of its eclectic appeal. Independent artists have transformed former souvenir shops into burlesque theaters and the public is invited to join the carnival with a summer festival and a Halloween walk. Surging foot traffic in the area has breathed new life into slightly creepy interpretations of classic performance arts including clowning and mime. At **Haley's Circus** (p52), traditional big-top entertainment is definitely alive and well with death-defying stunts performed by long-established carnival families. Comic relief can be a difficult art in itself, something you can learn first-hand in a visitor's session at **La Jeste Clown College** (p52). Offering classes in mime, juggling, illusion, stuntwork, physical comedy and more, La Jeste is one of the city's under-appreciated gems.

Classical and opera

There's no argument that the **Gotham City Opera House** (p52) is the city's premier venue for classic Italian commedia or German fairy-tale opera, but in recent years the former Vauxhall Concert Center has relaxed its repertoire to welcome stark stagings inspired by German Expressionism, as well as interactive multidiscipline experiments. The infusion of up-to-date technology, including holographic spotlights, continues to surprise traditionalists. The nearby **Josephine Hall** is home to the Gotham City Philharmonic, which frequently performs at public venues across the city, including the Fourth of July celebrations in Robinson Park.

The play's the thing

Theater Row (p53) is Midtown's cultural epicenter and a major attraction for out-of-towners visiting Gotham for the first time. Look out for bright posters and painted signs advertising the latest shows. The city often stages the first stateside interpretations of whatever productions are proving wildly popular in London's West End. If tickets are sold out at the theater's box office – as often happens – try the **Official Gotham City Information Center** (p62) on Chester Street. There you'll be first in line to buy unused tickets and enjoy exclusive visitor discounts.

The **Orpheum Theater** (p52) is the biggest of Theater Row's venues; many nearby restaurants offer dinner-and-a-show packages in conjunction with the venue. The venerable **Rosemont Theater** (p52) is a monument to local thespian history, with black and white lobby photos dating from the 1930s that showcase stars of the Rosemont stage over the decades.

Park Row had a shining theater hub in the 1930s, but economic downturns took their toll and the murders of Thomas and Martha Wayne nearly sealed the area's fate forever. Thankfully, the Wayne Foundation has made strides in resuscitating the district and the **Aragon Theater** (p51) is now a close match to its historical high point, and host of the Zorro Film Festival. The nearby **La Scala Theater** (p52) is a recently restored art deco movie-house palace.

Don't overlook the **Globe Theater** (p52), host of summer's A Week With Shakespeare festival (p25), which spills out from the theater itself on to the lawns of neighboring Robinson Park.

A sporting chance

The Midtown Arena is where basketball fans can watch the rising stars of the **Gotham Guardsmen** (p53). Football's **Gotham Goliaths** (p53) are a tough bunch and their fans are too, taking pride in the often-brutal weather conditions that lash Powers Stadium. Out in the suburb of Bristol is Blades Arena, home to hockey's **Gotham Blades** (p53), who have racked up five national championships for their city. Big crowds come into town for college football Saturdays to watch the **Gotham State University Wildcats** (p53), and GSU students have fielded top teams in other sports including softball and gymnastics.

Calendar

Volczek Festival

Plan your Gotham adventure in advance with our pick of the best annual events in the city. Dates and locations can change, so do check websites for up-to-date info before finalizing plans or check with the tourist office (p62) on Chester Street.

Spring

late Mar/early Apr **Easter Parade**
Old Gotham
www.gothameasterparade.got
Put on your Sunday best for this much-loved, old-fashioned Gotham City tradition. Attendees are often bedecked in throwback Victorian finery, while a costumed Easter Bunny tosses gold-wrapped chocolate coins to children.

mid Apr **Volczek Festival**
Little Odessa
www.volczekfestival.got
This signature event brings together all the immigrant communities within Little Odessa for a mutual exchange of music, food, drink, costuming, and dance. It's great fun for kids.

late Apr **Festival of St Leo**
Little Italy
www.festivalofstleo.got
The Little Italy neighborhood becomes a strollable, snackable feast during this week-long celebration honoring the Tuscan saint Leo the Great. Italian restaurants sell pastries and gelato on the strip of sidewalk adjacent to their buildings, with temporary overhangs forming a decorative canopy that protects noshers from spring showers. An open-air church service on Sunday evening closes the event.

early May **Museum Membership Drive**
Various venues
www.gothammuseums.got
A shared effort among Gotham's major museums to attract donations and sign up members. This two-week event sees late-night opening hours, new children's attractions, and the waiver of all admittance fees. The Natural History Museum and the Antiquities Museum are the biggest players, but check online for full listings.

Summer

early June **Food Fest**
Various venues
www.gothamfoodfest.got
This week-long festival started in Coventry, but now includes hundreds of restaurants in every corner of the city. Each venue offers up a special dinner at a fixed price, with $15, $25, and $35 tiers to reflect the exclusiveness of the cuisine. For many, there's no better opportunity to sample the fare offered by gourmand favorites such as the Blue Heron. Check the website for a full list of participants.

4 July **Fourth of July Fireworks Spectacular**
Various venues
www.julyfourthgotham.got
After dark, a fireworks barge anchored in the harbor near Blackgate launches the first pyrotechnics, kicking off a non-stop barrage that lasts about 30 minutes. Crowds gather along the Lower East Side waterfront in the late afternoon to grab the best views. Gotham's taller skyscrapers sell one-night observation packages.

late July **Gotham City Jazz Festival**
Burnley
www.gothamjazzfest.got
Bob your head to the sweet sounds of jazz as a four-block section of Burnley becomes a pedestrian plaza for the weekend. Big-name international stars turn up to jam alongside local groups.

mid Aug **A Week With Shakespeare**
Globe Theater & Robinson Park
www.gothamshakespearefest.got
The Globe Theater (of course) hosts this seven-day string of classics. All of the Bard's works are performed, but an overlapping schedule of indoor and outdoor performances makes it impossible for even the most devoted Shakespeare fan to see them all.

mid Aug **Carnivale**
Amusement Mile
www.gothamcarnivale.got
This celebration brings fresh crowds to the busy waterfront boardwalk at Amusement Mile. Parade floats, stunt performers, and trained animals are just a few of the sights in this home-grown event that has increased its attendance every year.

late Aug **Asylum**
Warehouse District
www.gothamasylumfest.got
For one weekend in August, the Warehouse District plays host to superstar DJs from around the world and thousands of sweaty EDM music devotees, for a sustained dose of sonic nirvana.

Autumn

early Sept **Burnley Arts Festival**
Little Bohemia
www.burnleyartsfest.got
This hipster favorite attracts thousands to the artists' enclaves scattered throughout the area informally known as Little Bohemia. Converted warehouses become stages for art exhibitions, indie film screenings, and interactive multimedia installations.

late Sept **Bowery Art Fair**
The Bowery
www.boweryartfair.got
More than 150 tents fill the blocked-off streets during this week-long gallery showcase for international and local artists. A must for art-lovers.

North Side Halloween Parade p26

Carnivale p25

early Oct **Wayne Foundation Half Marathon**
Midtown to Robinson Park
www.wfhalfmarathon.got
Benefiting multiple charities throughout the city, this popular run starts in Midtown and makes a scenic loop along the waterfront before finishing at the Nero Pavilion in Robinson Park.

31 Oct **North Side Halloween Parade**
Amusement Mile
www.gothamhalloweenparade.got
Amusement Mile's wooden boardwalk clatters under the footsteps of hundreds of revellers for this late-night spook fest. Zombies, living dolls, beastly hybrids, swamp monsters, and stitched-together patchwork people are just some of the scary sights on display for costume-watchers.

Winter

late Nov **Zorro Film Festival**
Park Row
www.zorrofilmfestival.got
Part of the Wayne Foundation's efforts to revive Park Row, this festival attracts film-lovers to sample an array of classic, foreign and independent films at the Aragon and La Scala theaters. Red-carpet premieres feature too.

mid Dec **Old Gotham Carols**
Old Gotham
www.oldgothamcarols.got
Hundreds of carolers gather on the steps of City Hall at sunset before bursting into song and making a two-hour circuit of Old Gotham's streets. Anyone is welcome to join in.

31 Dec **New Year's Eve**
Various locations
Gothamites count down the last night of the year in the Diamond District with a timer projected on to the side of the Ellsworth Building and an extravagant burst of celebratory fireworks. Swank, black-tie shindigs are held at the Iceberg Lounge and the Bristol Country Club, with tickets costing hundreds of dollars.

mid Jan **Garden Walk**
Wayne Botanical Garden
www.gothamgardenwalk.got
For four weekends of the year, the Wayne Botanical Garden decorates its exhibits in a seasonal theme and brings in live musicians and entertainers. The Winter Walk is the most popular of the four, offering a colorful respite from the post-holiday doldrums.

Feb **Chinese New Year**
Chinatown
www.gothamchinatown.got
Chinatown is festooned with colorful banners and illuminated by paper lanterns during the fortnight surrounding the Lunar New Year. Local restaurants put on special banquets. The evening street parades, complete with dragons and drummers, are a highlight.

17 Mar **St Patrick's Day Festival**
Port Adams
www.stpatsdaygotham.got
For over a century, crowds have filled the blocks near the Port Adams docks to raise a glass to the legacy of Gotham's Irish immigrants. Pubs in the area pool their resources to erect huge tents, where thirsty parade-goers are entertained by folk musicians.

Take to the streets

Get your glad rags on for Gotham's numerous street parades.

Seemingly everyone in Gotham loves a parade. In a city with a reputation for attracting oddballs, parades offer an excuse to don a costume and go a little crazy before returning to the humdrum of the workday nine-to-five.

Chinese New Year
Gotham's Chinatown neighborhood is at its most colorful and celebratory for two weeks in February. A street parade is held every evening, accompanied by musicians, popping firecrackers, and food carts. See p26.

Cinco de Mayo Festival
This citywide celebration of Latino culture rocks the Lower East Side with music, parties and a winding parade that invites spectators to join in the fun.

Easter Parade & Spring Celebration
The Easter Parade (p24) is the most popular part of this free celebration featuring children's activities, a petting zoo, an Easter bonnet contest, and flower displays from local garden clubs. The Easter Bunny brings up the rear of the parade, riding in a golden wagon and tossing sweets to spectators.

Festival of St Leo
This week-long April event (p24) is the best time to visit Little Italy. Performances of traditional Italian musicians, art exhibitions, and food specials fill the week. A respectfully reverent parade commemorates the life of the Tuscan saint.

Gotham City Pride
The last weekend of June is the time to celebrate diversity through music fests, a street fair, and educational conferences held in Kingston Square. Awards are handed out for parade floats and costumes based on creative interpretations of the festival's annual theme.

Independence Day Parade
More than 2,500 marchers and musicians parade through Old Gotham during July's Independence Day Parade. Expect Revolutionary War re-enactors, a pipe and drum corps, and readings of speeches by the Founding Fathers. Events wrap up by midday, leaving plenty of time to grab a good spot for watching the spectacular evening fireworks display.

St Patrick's Day Parade
First celebrated way back in 1799, the St Patrick's Day Festival (p26) turns Port Adams green every March. The festival kicks off on the Sunday before St Patrick's Day, while the parade starts in the Corktree neighborhood and proceeds – slightly drunkenly – down Kelly Street to the Port Adams pier.

Society Parade
Gotham's fraternal organizations date back to the 17th century. Today, more than 40 private outfits both open and secretive unite in May for this eclectic folk festival. Marchers play music and ride floats while promoting the virtues of their esoteric social clubs through outlandish attire and satirical takedowns of political figures.

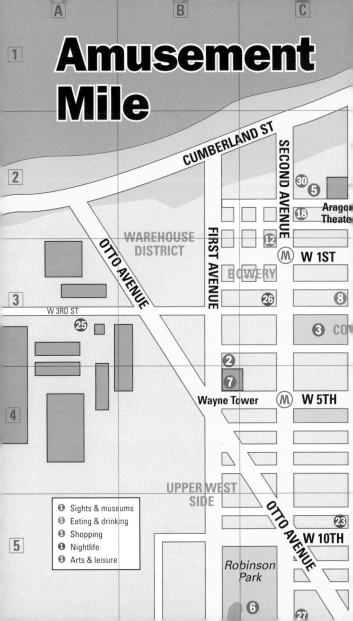

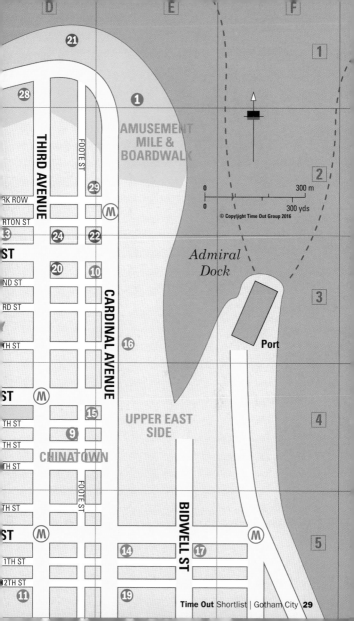

D
E
F

1

21

28

1

AMUSEMENT
MILE &
BOARDWALK

THIRD AVENUE

FOOTE ST

2

0   300 m

0   300 yds

© Copyright Time Out Group 2016

29

RK ROW

Ⓜ

RTON ST

24   **22**

3

*Admiral
Dock*

20   **10**

ST

ND ST

RD ST

CARDINAL AVENUE

TH ST

16

Port

3

ST   Ⓜ

TH ST

15

UPPER EAST
SIDE

4

TH ST

9

CHINATOWN

TH ST

TH ST

FOOTE ST

BIDWELL ST

ST   Ⓜ

Ⓜ

5

1TH ST

14   **17**

2TH ST

11

19

GOTHAM
HEIGHTS TOURS
EXPERIENCE THE OTHER SIDE OF GOTHAM!

GOTHAMHEIGHTSTOURS.GOT
800-555-1654

Gotham City

WAYNE ENTERPRISES

Amusement Mile

Sights & Museums

The ghosts of history seem to haunt Gotham City, with buildings bearing gothic spires and art deco adornments. Look up to take in the architecture, but don't expect to spot Gotham's urban legend, The Batman – even believers say the famed vigilante only comes out at night. The downtown edifices of Gotham, including **Wayne Tower**, the **Ellsworth Building**, the **Davenport Tower**, and the **Clocktower**, cast deep shadows at midday, and create an architectural court of kings. The city's museums are second to none, with world-class institutions that hold priceless masterpieces in their permanent collections and attract the best touring exhibits from around the globe. **Amusement Mile** on the north shore embraces its dark carnival reputation. In **Gotham Heights**, residents have converted parking garages into comfortably cozy wine bars. A great deal of Gotham has resisted industrial creep and is set aside for public use: the Reservoir in **Robinson Park** is ideal for weekend boating, while **Neo-Eden** and the **Wayne Botanical Garden** have pledged themselves to the celebration, and preservation, of natural greenery.

Amusement Mile

14 Cardinal Avenue. El Train B, C, D, E to Amusement Mile Station. **Open** 24hrs daily. **Admission** free. **Map** p28 E1 ❶
This long stretch on the north shore still boasts its original wooden board-walk erected in the 1910s. The glory days of the Amusement Mile were in the 1970s, but a bohemian revival in the last decade has brought in stunt shows and circus troupes, from Canada's Cirque des Planets and Europe's Cirque Sensationnel to the Haley Brothers acrobatics show. The renovated amusement park is a rollercoaster fan's

dream. Behind fences, sections of the park still await their facelifts, including the decaying Home of the Future, House of Mirrors and Tunnel of Love – popular visits for 'Urbex' practitioners and rumored hideouts for Gotham's notorious criminal, The Joker.

Arkham Asylum

W Merchant Street, at Salon Street (1-465 555 0111, www.arkhamasylum. got). El Train A, B, C, E to Tricorner Yards Station. Closed to the public.

The Victorian-style lines of the Elizabeth Arkham Asylum for the Criminally Insane attract architectural connoisseurs and history buffs alike – even though visitors are never allowed past the mansion's wrought-iron gates. A feature of Gotham since the early 1900s, the asylum took shape under the vision of Amadeus Arkham, who transformed his family estate into a treatment center for the mentally ill, until he too descended into madness. Visiting the gates of Arkham is officially discouraged by the city, but many can't resist snapping a photo of the (supposedly haunted) sanitarium that has housed The Joker, Killer Croc, and other notorious headline-grabbers.

Blackgate Penitentiary

Visible from shoreline along the Lower East Side. Closed to the public.

You can see this lonely island prison from the Gotham shoreline, but tours have been halted indefinitely following the most recent of Blackgate's frequent mass breakouts. At night, the spotlights of GCPD helicopters often illuminate the distant rock, and locals say this is your best chance to catch a glimpse of the so-called 'Batplane,' said to be the airborne transport of the city's Batman vigilante.

City Hall

Earl Street, at E Merchant Street (1-467 555 0102, www.gothamcityhall.got). El Train A, B, C, D to City Hall Station. **Tours** noon Tue-Thur. **Admission** free.

Construction began on City Hall in 1808 and was completed in 1819, with delays caused by war with the British in 1812. Tours of the historic edifice take visitors through the Lawmaker's Chamber and the Portrait Room.

Clocktower

W 4th Street, at First Avenue (1-467 555 0115, www.theclocktower. got). El Train A, B, C, D, E to Wayne Tower Station. **Open** By appointment. **Admission** free. **Map** p28 B3 **❷**

Constructed in 1938, the imposing Clocktower is owned by Wayne Enterprises, but has not housed any businesses in its lower levels since the gang war and urban unrest that tore the city in two in the 1970s. Bruce Wayne has committed the Wayne Foundation's charitable resources to the Clocktower's upkeep, and its chimes still mark the top of the hour to pedestrians across Gotham. The inner workings of the clock are viewable by appointment – it's popular, so best to book well ahead.

Ellsworth Building

Second Avenue, at Summit Lane (1-465 555 0152, www.ellsworth.got). El Train A, B, C, E to W 24th Street Station. **Open** 6am-10pm Mon-Sat. **Admission** $18; free-$12 reductions.

One of the city's distinctive skyscrapers, the Ellsworth Building opened in 1932 as the 'darling of the Diamond District.' The most iconic of its famed art deco designs is the enormous stylized face on one side, spanning several of the upper stories and looming large over pedestrians making their way up Second Avenue. Reservations for the observation deck can be made at the street-level ticket office. There's a small souvenir shop too.

Father Knickenbocker Wax Museum

W Merchant Street, at Merchant Street (1-467 555 0120, www.waxmuseum. got). El Train A, B, C to Marx Station.

Open 5-11pm Mon-Sat. **Admission** $18; free-$12 reductions.

This restored tenement building on the Lower West Side has lifelike wax figures cleverly posed in themed dioramas; look out for Marie Antoinette's aristocratic decadence, and the ghoulish horrors of Jack the Ripper. Historical Gotham names are also memorialized here, including industrialist Cameron Kane and surgeon Roger Elliot. The museum's most recent creations – contemporary Gothamites with their faces contorted in horror – have earned notoriety for their disturbingly realistic degree of detail.

Gotham City Museum of Antiquities

3431 Silva Parkway, at Cardinal Avenue (1-467 555 0127, www. gotham-museums.got/ant). El Train A, C, D, E to Park Street Station. **Open** 11am-9pm daily. **Admission** $26; $18 reductions.

The imposing Greek columns at the entrance speak to the grandeur of the treasures housed inside. For generations, Gotham's Museum of Antiquities has housed some of the world's rarest artifacts and also played host to touring exhibitions sharing the splendor of Islamic art, Classical Greece and the Italian Renaissance.

Gotham City Museum of Natural History

Cornerstone Court, at Horace Avenue (1-467 555 0128, www.gotham-museums.got/nh). El Train C, D to Jeremiah Avenue Station. **Open** 10am-9pm daily. **Admission** free.

A fixture of Old Gotham since the Civil War, the Natural History Museum displays rotating exhibits from its voluminous holdings in entomology, anthropology, zoology, and mineralogy. The dinosaur digs are a guaranteed hit with school children. The T-Rex in the central atrium nearly touches the ceiling, and some motorized dinos twitch and roar when visitors approach.

Gotham City Stock Exchange

2222 11th Street, at Third Avenue (1-465 555 0135, www.gotham stockexchange.got). El Train A, B, C, G to Financial District Station. **Open** 9am-4am Mon-Fri. **Admission** free.

If you're in the Financial District, don't forget a stop at the Stock Exchange. The trading bell rings at 9am, and the frenzied clamor of the traders is a stamp of the world's financial hubs. Adjacent is the (free) International Museum of Financial History, which has audio recollections by bankers hit hard by the stock market crash of 1929.

Gotham City Zoo

880 Second Avenue, at W 4th Street (1-465 555 0181, www.gothamzoo.got). El Train C, E, G to Coventry Station. **Open** *Apr-Oct* 10am-5pm Mon-Fri; 10am-6pm Sat, Sun. **Admission** $20; $12-$15 reductions. **Map** p28 C3 ❸

The venerable Gotham City Zoo began as a 'retirement home' for circus animals, giving aged lions, tigers, and elephants one last chance to entertain the crowds. Changing attitudes toward captive animals transformed the zoo in the 1990s, and its exhibits are now mostly cage-free re-creations of natural habitats. There is still a penguin beach, though, and a bat house.

Gotham Heights

El Train B, C, D to Gotham Heights Station.

Stroll this historic residential neighborhood and admire its splendid gothic architecture. Cathedral-like buildings, many of them crowned with pointed arches or supported by flying buttresses, are grand showcases for day spas and private social clubs.

Kane Art Museum

Jeremiah Avenue, at 11th Street (1-467 555 0134, www.kaneart.got). El Train C, D, E to Harbor Street Station. **Open** 11am-9pm Mon-Sat. **Admission** $28; free-$14 reductions.

A shrine to the contemporary arts, the Kane celebrates revolutionary creators and provocative works in architecture, photography, film, digital multimedia, and sequential art. Visit the gift shop for a quirky or inscrutable souvenir.

Neo-Eden

Earl Street, at W 5th Street (1-465 555 0112, www.neoeden.got). El Train A, B, C, D, E to Wayne Tower Station. **Open** 10am-11pm Mon-Sat. **Admission** $22; free-$14 reductions. **Map** p29 D4 ❹

The newest garden complex in Gotham City, Neo-Eden combines winding paths through tangles of snaking ivy with a spectacular enclosed hothouse that's home to thousands of exotic botanical species, including the largest collection of carnivorous plants in the world. Obtain medical advice before visiting, as the wild cocktail of pollen, spores, and pheromones given off by the plants has been known to trigger severe allergic reactions in some.

Park Row

Between Earl Street & Third Avenue. El Train C, D, E to Park Row Station. **Map** p28 C2 ❺

The Park Row community board has worked tirelessly over more than two decades to shed the borough's reputation as 'Crime Alley,' a nickname it acquired following the shocking murders of prominent Gothamites Thomas and Martha Wayne. Around-the-clock neighborhood watch and boosted GCPD patrols have resulted in a dramatic dip in street crime, though many people give the lion's share of the credit to the urban-legend vigilante known as The Batman.

Robinson Park

W 15th Street, at Second Avenue. El Train C, E, Q to Robinson Station. **Open** sunrise-sunset daily. **Admission** free. **Map** p28 C5 ❻

The oldest of Gotham's green spaces, Robinson Park has remained the city's wild heart for more than 200 years.

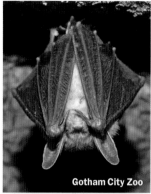

Gotham City Zoo

GOTHAM CITY

Its borders have withstood urban encroachment despite the real-estate premium on Central Island, and residents have long enjoyed boating or skating on the reservoir or sunning themselves on the west lawn when springtime temps finally hit 'shorts weather.' Landmarks include the neo-Roman architecture of the Forum of the Twelve Caesars, the landscaped mound that hides the old Johnson Landfill, Giella Gardens, and Finger Castle, an eccentric residence built in the 1860s and now operated by the Gotham Historical Society.

Tricorner Park

W Merchant Street, at Tricorner Street. El Train A, B, C, E to Tricorner Yards Station. **Open** sunrise-sunset daily. **Admission** free.

This smallish shoreline park is known for its esplanade, a wide lane along the waterfront restricted to pedestrian and bicycle traffic. Benches offer a relaxing view of the harbor, but become makeshift bunks for vagrants after sunset.

Wayne Botanical Garden

450 Park Street, at McGee Street (1-465 555 0176, www.waynegarden.got). El Train A, B, D, E to Drummond Court Station. **Open** 11am-10pm Mon-Sat. **Admission** $20; free-$12 reductions.

Founded by Martha Wayne, the Wayne Botanical Garden continues its mission to make natural beauty accessible to all of Gotham's citizens. Open year round, the garden is a showcase for new developments from Wayne Biotech, with color-shifting roses and flowers that bloom in the winter snow.

Wayne Tower

220 W 5th Street, at First Avenue (www.wayneenterprises.got). El Train A, B, C, D, E to Wayne Tower Station. Closed to the public. **Map** p28 B4 **7**

Wayne Enterprises, Gotham City's backbone since the 19th century, built an empire on real estate, railroads and oil, though the lineage of famous Waynes traces even further back to fur traders swapping pelts with the French. The family company is currently embodied by billionaire Bruce Wayne, the most famous man in Gotham. Wayne Tower is the company's headquarters looming over the city; the spire are said to guard the entrances to Gotham. The building is a popular photo-op, but access is restricted to employees. Nevertheless, as the company's branches include Wayne Biotech, Wayne Aerospace, Wayne Chemicals, Wayne Shipping, Wayne Steel, and Wayne Foods, it's virtually impossible to spend an afternoon in Gotham and not see the Wayne logo in your dreams when you finally drift off to sleep.

Wayne Botanical Garden

Eating & Drinking

After centuries as a port city, it's no wonder that Gotham is famous for its seafood. The docks at Port Adams are home to a veritable armada of commercial fishermen, who offload freshly netted catches to restaurant wholesalers within minutes of arriving into port. Eateries near the waterfront attract top seafood chefs and provide dazzling views of the ocean horizon. But it's not all fishy fare: many other cuisines are represented in Gotham, from the family-owned kitchens of Chinatown to the hearty Slavic fare in Little Odessa. French cuisine, spurred by an influx of moneyed European emigrés, is also making a comeback following the Francophile fad's collapse a decade ago. Pizzas, burgers, and family-style classics are easy to find, but don't believe every street-level sign that promises to provide Gotham's 'best' or 'most authentic' dishes.

Big Belly Burger

Multiple locations (1-467 555 0195, www.bigbellygotham.got). **Open** 6am-11pm daily. **$. Burgers**
Big Belly started in Coast City, but the chain's acquisition by LexCorp has led to franchises popping up all along the Eastern Seaboard. Gothamites are arguably the most loyal Big Belly fans of them all, with more than 20 locations within the Gotham city limits. Regional favorites on the custom menu include the Dent Double and the Wayne Steakburger. On the back of the paper placemats is an El Train network map.

Blue Heron

520 Earl Street, at W 3rd Street (1-465 555 0188, www.blueheron.got). El Train C, E, G to Coventry Station. **Open** 11am-midnight daily. **$$$. Eclectic Map** p28 C3 ⑧
The cliquish air of Coventry suits the Blue Heron, one of Gotham's most venerable five-star restaurants, with

Bristol Country Club

decor inspired by the beaded, ostrich-feather elegance of the Roaring Twenties. There's little need to study the standard menu when the specials feature such adventurous and delectable entrees as Sinaloan *pescado zarandeado* and perfectly prepped *uni*. The Blue Heron is famous for its 'desserts only' date-night package, offered just once a year on Valentine's Day.

Bristol Country Club

5542 Thurston Street, at Fifth Avenue (1-465 555 0165, www.bristolcountry dub.got). El Train A, B, D, E to Drummond Court Station. **Open** 10am-1am Mon-Sat. **$$$. Steakhouse**
This surf-and-turf palace has been attracting Gotham celebs since the 1940s and still retains a timeless air of post-war sophistication. Jackets and ties are mandatory for gentlemen, while tuxedos are needed for big-ticket annual events such as the New Year's Eve Fete and the GCPD Million Dollar Memorial Fundraiser. Forward-thinking drinks include mezcal and soju cocktails, but for dinner, stick with the classics, such as the butter-seared flank steak, cooked to perfection.

Chinatown

Around W 7th Street & Foote Street (1-465 555 0195, www.gotham chinatown.got). El Train A, B, E, Q to Chinatown Station. **Open** varies. **$-$$$. Asian** Map p29 D4 ❾
The Red Lotus (p41) is just one of dozens of authentic Asian eateries to be found in Chinatown. Take your pick from the high-tech automation of Mecha Sushi and the smoky food stands that line the alleyways of Butchers Block. Exotic delicacies such as jellied eel and century eggs appeal to the adventurous palate. Enter Chinatown through the archway at Storrow and Foote Streets, or stroll over to the Hmong-owned carts that are lined up along Englehart.

Ciao Bella

982 Cardinal Avenue, at W Second Street (1-465 555 0132, www.ciaobella.got). El Train B, C, D, E to Amusement Mile Station. **Open** 11am-1am Mon-Sat. **$$. Italian** Map p29 D3 ❿
Without a heads-up, you might walk right past Ciao Bella, but once inside, the restaurant is stunning. With a softly lit bar (the cocktails are inspired and unorthodox) and dark woodwork throughout, this is sexy, modern Italian. Diners are encouraged to share everything on the small-plates menu, from the cold and hot antipasti to the main dishes. Try the Roman *suppli*, the squash blossoms, and the whole *branzino*. All tables are good tables, and the kitchen doesn't close until last call.

Jitters

Falcone's

*505 Bidwell Street, at E Merchant Street
(1-467 555 0177, www.falcones.got).
El Train B, C, D to Darby Station.* **Open**
4pm-midnight Mon-Sat. **$$**. **Italian**
Falcone's has been family-owned since
1950, though the family in question –
the rumored Mafioso cabal currently
headed by Sofia Falcone-Gigante – is
the stuff of Gotham crime legend.
Don't worry, you can expect bresaola
instead of bullets (although staring
too long at the corner booths might
be ill-advised). The menu here has
remained unchanged since it opened,
with Sofia seemingly subscribing to
her father Carmine's motto that 'some-
times, the old ways are best.'

Finger Foods

*242 W 15th Street, at Otto Avenue
(1-467 555 0138, www.fingerfoods
gotham.got). El Train C, E, Q to Robinson
Station.* **Open** 5pm-1am Mon-Sat. **$$**.
Tapas
Proximity to the Theater District
has made this contemporary take
on Spanish tapas a don't-miss weekend experience for many. Highlights
among the many cold and hot small-
plate delicacies are lamb meatballs in
plum sauce, tortilla with red onions
and goat cheese, and *patatas bravas*
with a piquant sauce. Sherry lovers will
be delighted by the range.

Fox Gardens

*Third Avenue, at W 12th Street
(1-465 555 0187, www.foxgardens.got).
El Train A, B, C to W 10th Street Station.* **Open** 4pm-midnight daily. **$$$**.
Eclectic Map p29 D5 ⓫
In less than a decade, this impressive
addition to Midtown has built a reputa-
tion as the quintessential spot for mar-
riage proposals or post-awards bashes.
Reservations are required and the wait-
ing list is long; it's recommended that
you book at least a month in advance.
The lounge features a piano player and
private table service, and the maître
d' doesn't crowd the floor, making it a
pleasantly peaceful environment for
discreet conversation.

Jitters

*Multiple locations (1-467 555 0106,
www.jittersgotham.got).* **Open** 6am-
10pm daily. **$**. **Café Map** p28 C3 ⓬
This coffeehouse took root in the
Bowery and has sprouted branches
across the country, making it as far as
Central City, but in Gotham it's a proud
local institution. Jitters roasts and
packages its own third party-certified
organic coffee, and the baristas take
their jobs seriously. Try the Harrar, and
the Jamaica Blue Mountain, roasted
on-site. At the original Bowery loca-
tion, take a peek through the glass
partition behind the counter at Jitters'
giant roasters.

Luigi's Pizza

*312 Barton Street, at King Street (1-465
555 0122, www.luigispizza.got). El Train
C, D, E to Park Row Station.* **Open** 10am-
11pm daily. **$**. **Pizza Map** p29 D2 ⓭
Luigi's Pizza wasn't founded by an
actual Luigi, but rest assured that the
pizzas are authentic Napoli delicacies.
Thin crust, shredded parmesan, and a
sweetly spicy tomato sauce are trade-
marks of a Luigi's pie. The tables are
covered in butcher paper, with crayons
supplied for kids to play hangman.
The spot is usually packed with a mix
of families, college kids, and locals

GOTHAM CITY

A STAR ALLIANCE MEMBER
WIDEN YOUR WORLD
TURKISH AIRLINES
NOW FLYING TO GOTHAM CITY
#FLYTOGOTHAM

satisfying their urge for a quick slice. Try the taco, buffalo chicken, and spaghetti and meatball varieties.

MM Good Donuts

2285 Park Street, at Cornerstone Court (1-465 555 0151, www.mmgooddonuts. got). El Train A, C, D, E to Park Street Station. **Open** 5am-4pm daily. **$**. **Diner**
It sounds counter-intuitive, but MM Donuts is as much about the burritos as it is about donuts and coffee (though they brew Pumpworks). Gothamites eat burritos like it's their last meal on death row – take it to-go or eat in at MM's counter. Space is limited, but you won't have long to wait. The donuts (especially the matcha longjohns and earl gray crullers) are great too.

Pamela's Café

801 Bidwell Street, at 11th Street (1-467 555 0192, www.pamelas.got). El Train A, B, C, G to Financial District Station. **Open** 24hrs daily. **$**. **Café**
The *Gotham Freepress* hails Pamela's for the 'best breakfast in Gotham City,' and the lines around the block on weekends prove that the reviewers are on to something. Its 24-7 hours and central location in the Financial District make this neon-lit spot popular with both church-going families and bar-hopping night owls. The smothered buttermilk biscuit is a must-try, and free coffee is provided for line-waiters.

Paradise Club

876 Cardinal Avenue, at W 11th Street (1-465 555 0106, www.paradisedub. got). El Train A, B, C to W 10th Street Station. **Open** 4pm-2am Mon-Sat. **$$**. **Bar/Cajun Map** p29 E5 ⑭
Gotham's home for New Orleans-style jazz, the Paradise Club serves up seriously spicy Cajun cuisine to match the hot tones of its trumpet soloist. Belly up to the bar for a shot of liquorice whiskey before tucking into a tin bucket filled with freshly steamed crawdads. Don't miss the jambalaya.

Red Lotus

333 Foote Street, at W 6th Street (1-465 555 0109, www.redlotus.got). El Train A, B, E, Q to Chinatown Station. **Open** 10am-midnight daily. **$$**. **Asian Map** p29 D4 ⑮
The Red Lotus is Gotham City's definitive Chinatown dining experience, with five levels each boasting its own cultural menu and devoted fanbase. The Thai, Chinese, Japanese, Korean, and Vietnamese floors don't seem to suffer from this stratification, though, thanks to owner Koh Jian's insistence on hiring chefs who source their own ingredients. The Red Lotus offers a surprisingly deep vegan menu.

Riverside Lounge

440 Cardinal Avenue, at W 4th Street (1-467 555 0105, www.riverside lounge.got). El Train A, B, E, Q to Chinatown Station. **Open** 10am-1am daily. **$$**. **Bar Map** p29 E3 ⑯
The Riverside Lounge boasts of its gangster heritage with black and white wall murals depicting Prohibition-era bootlegging – punctuated with crimson splashes in scenes of tommy-gun executions. Recently refurbished, the Lounge now caters to an upscale crowd, with well-dressed walk-ins cozying up to rye-based drinks. Don't miss the Green Fairy and her absinthe cart, supplying the famous bohemian drink to patrons throughout the night.

Tap Room

58 Bidwell Street, at W 11th Street (1-465 555 0122, www.taproom.got). El Train B, E to Temple Station. **Open** 3pm-2am Mon-Sat. **$$**. **Bar/Barbecue Map** p29 E5 ⑰
What's on tap at the Tap Room? Beer and ribs, and what the menu lacks in variety is more than compensated for with A+ quality. Taking up most of a city block, this restaurant/brewery has more than 70 drafts on tap and nearly 1,000 imported and domestic bottles ready for order. Don't miss the spice-seared baby back ribs.

GOTHAM CITY

Midtown Mall p44

Shopping

Gotham has a deserved reputation as an unmatched hub for vintage fashion. The city's designers often unveil retro-inspired ensembles on the runways, and thrift stores are plentiful. But a classic look doesn't require an outdated attitude, so don't be surprised to see a tattoo sleeve poking out of the business man's suit next to you on the El Train. Dressing yourself head to foot in the nostalgic Gotham style is easy, thanks to a **Fashion District** that caters to tastemakers like supermodel Mari Jiwe McCabe, as well as urban and suburban malls that offer steep discounts for the masses.

In Gotham's **Diamond District**, where second-hand steals share space with one-of-a-kind dazzlers, you'll find a similar range in the selection of precious stones and settings. **Kingston Square** is an amiable microcosm of the college experience with coffeehouses and

bars in equal measure, while the **Electronics Sector** is the place to unearth imported gadgets that have yet to make the jump to the U.S. mainstream. Throughout Gotham City it is impossible to ignore the parade of odd, quirky or just plain inexplicable stores that seem to exist only here. Don't worry how these curiosities stay in business, just walk through the door and soak up the strangeness.

10/6
319 W 20th Street, at Third Avenue (1-465 555 0193, www.ten-six.got). El Train B, D to W 20th Street Station.
Open 11am-9pm Mon-Sat.
10/6's wooden sign has hung on W 20th Street since 1919, remaining unchanged as the store has shifted its focus away from mass appeal to specialize in vintage curiosities and theatrical supplies. Most of the stock consists of exuberant ladies'

bonnets and silk-lined men's bowlers, but contemporary shoppers can also buy sports-logoed baseball caps or knitted ski caps during Gotham's sudden cold snaps. Maybe it's only due to hipsters' love of vintage headgear, but the customers seem rabid enough to be brainwashed. Don't miss out.

Alice's Antiques

202 Barton Street, at Second Avenue (1-467 555 0170, www.alices.got). El Train C, D, E to Park Row Station. **Open** 11am-9pm daily. **Map** p28 C2 ⑬
A quaint Victorian storefront invites you to explore three levels of curiosities linked by a spiral staircase. Clothing, furniture, toys, and grooming accessories from the 19th century can be found in this charmingly old-fashioned reproduction of a bygone age.

Davenport Center

Cardinal Avenue, at W 12th Street (1-467 555 0122, www.davenportcenter. got). El Train A, B, C to W 10th Street Station. **Open** 9am-9pm daily. **Map** p29 E5 ⑲

This is one of Gotham City's tallest skyscrapers, and its six lowest floors are devoted to shopping. An emphasis on womenswear makes it ideal for browsing designer dresses, globally sourced imports, handcrafted jewelry, leather accessories and totes. Upscale beauty products include striking nail polishes, lipsticks and eyeshadows.

Diamond District

Blocks N of Summit Lane & W of Earl Street (www.gothamdiamonddistrict. got). El Train A, B, C, D, E, G to Diamond District Station.
Impossibly exquisite jewelry boutiques, precious metal resellers, and cash-flashing pawn shops all share the Diamond District's busy streets. Institutions such as Balthazar's specialize in rare gemstones and intricate metalworking. Many shops here have crafted jaw-dropping custom pieces for celebrities and billionaires.

Electronics Sector

First Avenue, at 10th Street (www. gothamelectronicssector.got).

Alice's Antiques

GOTHAM CITY

Diamond District p43

El Train B, C, D to 8th Street Station.
The intersection of First Avenue and Tenth Street is the cross hairs of the city's Electronics Sector, so named after goliath computer retailer Gem Electronics opened its three-story, glass and steel shrine to personal technology in the 1980s. Today, a stripped-down Gem offers refurbished mobile devices and discount entertainment downloads. Smaller pop-ups sell hip gadgets and personalized accessories imported direct from Tokyo's Akihabara District.

Fashion District

Blocks N of Summit Lane & W of Bidwell Street (1-465 555 0178, www. gothamfashiondistrict.got). El Train B, D to W 20th Street Station.
Midtown's Fashion District is the nexus of cutting-edge haute couture, and steep discounts on designer labels and last season's runway favorites. Admiring the window displays on Raciette Avenue doesn't cost a dime, but the style-conscious will find it hard to leave the neighborhood without dropping some cash.

Kingston Square

11th Street, at First Avenue (1-465 555 0137, www.kingstonsquare.got). El Train B, C, D, E, G, Q to Kingston Square Station.
A few blocks from the Gotham State University campus, Kingston Square is a hub of bookstores, coffee shops, pizza parlors, happy-hour dive bars, and music shops selling vintage vinyl and retro fashion. Prices are rock-bottom.

Midtown Mall

895 W 20th Street, at Bidwell Street (1-465 555 0149, www.midtownmall. got). El Train B, D to W 20th Street Station. **Open** 9am-9pm daily.
A shopping mecca popular with suburbanites and out-of-towners, Midtown Mall features 120 stores on three levels. Attractions include factory-discount clothiers, footwear and accessory outlets, and a 20-screen movie theater.

Zatara's Magic Shop

3508 Earl Street, at 8th Street (1-467 555 0190, www.zatarasmagicshop.got). El Train B, C, D to 8th Street Station. **Open** 11am-11pm Mon-Sat.
The top-hatted sign marks the doorway to Zatara's, which has offered equipment and advice for the magicians' community since 1938. It sells everything from linking rings to vanishing cabinets, and also doubles as a museum of the magical arts. Attention, ghost hunters: many unexplained happenings, supposedly triggered by supernatural energies, have been linked to this address.

Suburban malls

There are also plenty of bargains to be had at the malls in Greater Gotham. Family-friendly **Castleland Mall** has an enclosed amusement park, a hands-on children's museum and a popular food court, while **Richland Mall** targets bargain-conscious fashionistas with boutiques, galleries, and French pastry shops. The **Crystal Palace** advertises itself as 'America's Mall,' though its 200 high-end shops are geared toward the deep-pocketed. Gargantuan, *Nutcracker*-inspired marionettes are hung above Santa's Village here from Thanksgiving through New Year's Day.

Leader of the pack

The story of Gotham City is the story of Wayne Enterprises.

No company has meant more to Gotham's history or done more to shape Gotham's future than Wayne Enterprises. A diverse megacorporation active in dozens of countries across the world, it still honors its Gotham roots by funnelling much of its wealth into local development.

Wayne Enterprises can trace its origins back centuries to fur traders who occupied the fort in what is now Old Gotham. The Wayne family crafted an empire in the 19th century, first with real estate and transatlantic shipping, and later with railroads and oil.

Over 30 years ago a mugger gunned down company president Thomas Wayne and his wife Martha in a Park Row alley. A shocked city floundered for a decade until orphaned heir Bruce Wayne finally took the helm and charted a new course.

Today, Wayne Enterprises is leading the charge into new frontiers including nanotechnology and genetic engineering. With Bruce Wayne as CEO and Lucius Fox as business manager, the various divisions of Wayne Enterprises – listed below – have seen unprecedented success.

Wayne Aerospace
Second only to Ferris Air, Wayne Aerospace manufactures both private jets and commercial airliners and supplies experimental aircraft to NASA. Its engine prototypes using new-wave smart materials are said to be years ahead of their time.

Wayne Biotech
Success at sequencing the human genome led Wayne Biotech to market new cures and to introduce better training for hospital workers. A few of the side benefits from Wayne Biotech's research into plant life – such as color-changing roses – are on display in the exotic Wayne Botanical Garden (p36).

Wayne Chemicals
Wayne Chemicals started in the 1950s as a supplier to petrochemical industries in the Burnley district. Today, the division works with Wayne Pharmaceuticals to synthesize vaccines. It is credited with ending the city's mysterious 'fear gas' outbreak.

Wayne Foundation
The charitable arm of Wayne Enterprises makes its influence felt all over the city, from the renovations in Park Row to the free medical clinics that offer care to anyone in need, pumping millions into worthy causes. The Wayne Foundation is also a major supporter of Gotham's arts and culture scene.

Wayne Technologies
Miniaturized gadgets and orbital satellites aren't the only futuristic things being dreamed up in WayneTech's classified 'clean room' labs. WayneTech's long-running rivalry with Lex Luthor's LexCorp and Ted Kord's Kord Industries means that the division never allows itself to sit still.

27 Tek

Nightlife

Gotham City's gritty soul is what gives its nightlife such electric authenticity. The waterfront and the Diamond District are home to gentlemen's clubs and retro speakeasies, where old-money luminaries sip dry martinis and toast the city's bright future. Venture out into the fringes and you'll find a Gotham that's both dangerous and thrilling. After 1am, you can't miss the city's heartbeat when the sidewalk starts vibrating with the thump-thump-thump of heavy bass.

Old-schoolers such as DJ Kiteman mix it up on the West Side, while up-and-comers like K-Lown light up the Bowery. Abandoned buildings in the Warehouse District and Robbinsville have been converted by locals into paint-splattered, vibrant celebrations of rave culture, though out-of-towners are advised to keep their wallets close and to travel with a friend. Amusement Mile is the city's home for burlesque – performed against the backdrop of a crowded carnival boardwalk – while Burnley Harbor (aka Little Bohemia) captures the city's dynamic arts scene.

27 Tek

232 Third Avenue, at W 1st Street (1-465 555 0138, www.27tek.got). El Train B, C, D, E to Amusement Mile Station. **Open** 10pm-4am Mon-Sat. **Map** p29 D3 ⓴
Voted 'best club' three years in a row by Gotham's independent press, 27 Tek is known for its pristine sound quality. The club limits attendance to guarantee that all patrons have the best experience possible. Doors open at 10pm, but lines often start forming at 8pm.

Amusement Mile Burlesque

N of Cumberland Street & E of Cardinal Avenue. El Train B, C, D, E to Amusement Mile Station. **Open** varies. **Map** p29 E2 ㉑

Seasonal storefronts along the Amusement Mile Boardwalk (p32) have found surprising life as playful showcases for the art of burlesque. Classically trained ballet artists and leggy acrobats strut their stuff on dimly lit stages, performing routines that would feel right at home in your great-grandfather's era. Primping pin-up girls and glam divas circulate through the audience, making everyone a part of the bawdy fun.

Circo Roma

Cardinal Avenue, at W 1st Street (1-467 555 0191, www.circoroma.got). El Train B, C, D, E to Amusement Mile Station. **Open** 7pm-2am Mon-Sat. **Map** p29 E3 ㉒

Just a block south of Amusement Mile, this circus-themed nightclub is shunned by outsiders spooked by the neighborhood's bad reputation. As a result, it has become a firm favorite with locals. Circo Roma's faded posters of lion tamers and freak-show exhibits are a prelude to the main event: a vibrant, multimedia assault of spinning, hallucinatory holograms and calliope-tinged dance music.

Club Vesuvius

Cornerstone Court, at Jeremiah Avenue (1-467 555 0109, www.clubvesuvius.got). El Train C, D to Jeremiah Avenue Station. **Open** 10pm-4am Mon-Sat.

Vesuvius, which has reopened its doors following an arson scare, is fast becoming a must-visit for both Gothamites and out-of-towners. The club wears its 1940s styling with pride, thanks to owner (and famously 'reformed' mobster) Johnny Sabatino. Call ahead if you want to catch the mind-boggling magic of Zatanna, a regular here.

Egyptian

2132 Earl Street, at W 10th Street (1-465 555 0197, www.theegyptian.got). El Train A, B, C to W 10th Street Station. **Open** 5pm-2am Mon-Fri; 5pm-4am Sat. **Map** p28 C5 ㉓

Golden statues of the cat goddess Bast guard the entrance to the Egyptian, a purr-fect addition to the city's after-hours scene. Don't expect to get in unless you're wearing semi-formal attire, but once inside the attentive wait staff will make you feel like a million bucks all night long. Sultry lounge music and a brandy bar are highlights of this hangout favored by Gotham's young and wealthy.

Gotham City Olympus

Horace Avenue, at 11th Street (1-465 555 0147, www.gothamcityolympus.got). El Train C, D, E to Harbor Street Station. **Open** 24hrs daily.

One of two casinos run by eccentric Gotham industrialist Maxie Zeus, the Olympus offers Monte Carlo-style table games, with bets starting at $500. Perks such as theater tickets and bottles of rare champagne are plentiful for high rollers. The casino's private security force maintains order and will forcibly eject the newly bankrupt. The casino plays host to high-profile MMA fights, but old-school boxing is still big business, harkening back to the glory days of heavyweights like Ted 'Wildcat' Grant.

Gramercy Loft

892 Cornerstone Court, at Merchant Street (1-465 555 0134, www.gramercyloft.got). El Train B, C, D, E to Cornerstone Station. **Open** 8pm-2am Mon-Sat.

The best place in the city to catch unsigned bands before they break, the Gramercy offers two levels of entertainment and a seasonal roof deck. This renovated warehouse is much loved by the Gotham State U crowd, quickly filling to capacity on Friday and Saturday nights.

Iceberg Lounge

Cornerstone Court, at Harbor Street (1-465 555 0144, www.iceberglounge.got). El Train C, D to Jeremiah Avenue Station. **Open** 7pm-3am Mon-Sat.

Few visitors to Gotham City can resist the temptation to spend a night at the Iceberg Lounge. This trendy, stylish club is the coolest new addition to the city scene, occupying a prime piece of waterfront real estate that offers stunning views of the harbor from a sprawling, two-story restaurant and lounge. Owner Oswald Cobblepot – Gotham's infamous 'Penguin' – indulges his quirks with an umbrella stand at the door and a chilled pool in the dining area where seals and waterfowl cavort. Big-band standards are the rule on the dancefloor, and the Iceberg's New Year's Eve party is already the stuff of legend. For those with the cash, the VIP dining area on the upper floor offers private entertainment and the chance to spot rumored criminal scions from the Falcone and Maroni families.

Kremlin Klub

8th Street, at Harbor Street (1-465 555 0185, www.kremlinklub.got). El Train C, D, E to Harbor Street Station. **Open** 8pm-3am Mon-Sat.

During the Cold War, the Little Odessa neighborhood was a supposed hive of Soviet spies and KGB enforcers. The legend receives a hipster's twist in the Kremlin Klub, a two-level dance venue spinning eastern European EDM. Stark cement walls are adorned with Mother Russia memorabilia. Security cameras are everywhere – even the toilet stalls – as a (hopefully) ironic nod to the USSR's surveillance state. Come for the music and a bite-sized taste of Brutalist architecture.

Maxie's Casino

Third Avenue, at W 1st Street (1-465 555 0103, www.maxiescasino.got). El Train B, C, D, E to Amusement Mile Station. **Open** 24hrs daily. **Map** p28 D3 ㉔

The smaller sister of Gotham City Olympus (p47) is optimized for the masses. Rows of burbling slot machines and $5 gaming tables offer low-stakes thrills, while the live entertainment leans toward nostalgia acts

from the past. Gamblers drink for free, but generous tips are encouraged.

Peregrinator's Club

689 Cornerstone Court, at Park Street (1-465 555 0198, www.peregrinators. got). El Train A, C, D, E to Park Street Station. **Open** Members 5pm-1am Mon-Sat. *Tours* noon 3rd Sun of mth.

This explorer-themed club is an undisputed art deco masterpiece. Built in 1932, it bears jazz-age architectural angles and streamlined sculptures of brass falcons perched atop stylized globes. Club major-domo Ronald Edwards hosts guided tours one Sunday a month. Bluebloods such as Bruce Wayne are lifetime Peregrinator members, but don't expect to spot them on tour days. The cocktail menu has remained unchanged (bar the prices) since it opened.

Sionis Below

Otto Avenue, at W 3rd Street (location varies at short notice). **Map** p28 A3 ㉕

According to rumor, this stripped-down sweatbox in the Warehouse District is cover for a bare-knuckled, amateur fight club – but its owners and loyal patrons remain tight-lipped. The club has no posted hours, no phone, no website and it changes location semi-monthly. Get directions from someone you trust, and prepare yourself for a memorable night.

Tobacconists Club

420 Electric Street, at Silva Parkway (1-465 555 0100, www.tobacconistsclub. got). El Train C, D to Jeremiah Avenue Station. **Open** 4pm-1am Mon-Sat.

Founded as a members-only club during Gotham City's postwar industrial boom, the Tobacconists Club opened to the public 20 years ago to combat a membership decline and capitalize on the then-hot cigar craze. In its cozy environs you can relax in leather easy chairs while staring out the bay windows at the illuminated Gotham skyline. The dark, mahogany decor

Maxie's Casino

is best experienced through a smoky haze amid the strains of a jazz band. Without a jacket and tie – or an evening gown for the ladies – don't expect to get past the front door.

Ventriloquist Club

427 Electric Street, at Cornerstone Court (1-467 555 0172, www.ventriloquistclub. got). El Train C, D to Jeremiah Avenue Station. **Open** 7pm-2am Mon-Sat.
This Lower Gotham nightspot is a notoriously random entertainment venue. You're just as likely to see vaudeville routines and stand-up comedy as you are to bliss out to trance EDM or participate in a 'living art' exhibit. Getting past the hulking bouncer is a feat in itself. Owner Arnold Wesker has

packed the lobby (and the bathrooms) with glass cases housing ventriloquism props, making the club a vintage museum honoring this strange art.

Victorian Parlor

280 W 3rd Street, at Second Avenue (1-465 555 0123, www.victorianparlor. got). El Train C, E, G to Coventry Station. **Open** 5pm-2am Mon-Sat. **Map** p28 C3 ㉖
Most Lower Bowery residents agree that the Victorian Parlor is a fitting addition to Gotham's proud tradition of elegant creepiness. Inside, hostesses in corsets and hoop skirts usher patrons to lounging couches, to sip absinthe and puff on hookahs. A pipe organ is intentionally kept out of tune to evoke an aura of minor-key dread.

Orpheum Theater p52

Arts & Leisure

There's always plenty of fun kicking up in Gotham, from a surging theater scene to an indie-arts incubator in the paint-splattered lofts of Little Bohemia. The **Gotham City Opera House** and the **Rosemont Theater** are twin cornerstones of culture for the highbrow set, and are architectural draws even for those who don't care about seeing the latest shows. In Park Row, the theaters have bounced back after the decades-long street-crime panic triggered by the Wayne murders, with an increased police presence and a can-do attitude from the Park Row locals.

Amusement Mile's boardwalk may be past its prime, but Gotham's carnival heritage is alive and well in places such as **Haley's Circus** and the historic **La Jeste Clown College**. And if pro sports are your game, Gotham is proud of its newly modernized athletic arenas for showdowns in basketball,

football, and hockey. There's no bandwagon-jumping in Gotham – its residents are fiercely loyal to their hometown teams, no matter their win/loss record.

Aragon Theater

150 Park Row, at Earl Street (1-465 555 0133, www.aragontheater.got). El Train C, D, E to Park Row Station.

A multimillion-dollar renovation led by the Wayne Foundation has transformed the Aragon and surrounding blocks – it's a giant step toward ridding the area of its 'Crime Alley' image. Even though Bruce Wayne admits there's still work to be done, the restored theater and the El Train pass-over alleys are cleaner and better lit than they were in the dismal era that saw the fatal muggings of Wayne's parents, Thomas and Martha. Business plummeted in the aftermath of that tragedy, but the Aragon now lures hundreds of customers with themed movie nights and screenings

GOTHAM CITY

for local filmmakers and videographers. Annual film fests dedicated to various Zorro incarnations and the films of Fritz Lang are big draws.

Globe Theater

Second Avenue, at W 15th Street (1-465 555 0108, www.globetheater.got). El Train C, E, Q to Robinson Station. **Map** p28 C5 ㉗

Named in honor of Shakespeare's Elizabethan haunt – but not patterned after it architecturally – the Globe Theater sits at the edge of Robinson Park. It is the home for Shakespeare adaptations, children's theater performances and touring musical acts. Audience members are frequently pulled on stage to join in the action.

Gotham City Opera House

1665 Earl Street, at Cornerstone Court (1-465 555 0154, www.gothamcity operahouse.got). El Train B, C, D, E to Cornerstone Station.

The grand dame of Gotham's performance spaces, the former Vauxhall Concert Center is today the city's Opera House. A neo-baroque hymn to celebratory ostentation, the Opera House offers architectural tours of its lobby, vestibules, and the painted ceiling in the auditorium. Critically praised productions have included *Lucia di Lammermoor*, *L'Orfeo* and *Orfeo ed Euridice*. Many patrons of the Opera House, including Bruce Wayne, hold season tickets, making seats sometimes tricky to secure for visitors with limited planning time – though your hotel concierge may be able to help.

Haley's Circus

290 Third Avenue, at Cumberland Street (1-467 555 0179, www.haleyscircus.got). El Train B, C, D, E to Amusement Mile Station. **Map** p29 D1 ㉘

Family-owned Haley's Circus has been welcoming crowds inside the big top for generations. Haley's offers the traditional three rings of entertainment, but emphasizes human feats over animal acts. Trapeze and high-wire artists, contortionists and magicians serve up an unforgettable spectacle. Acrobats the Flying Graysons – famously killed in a fall before a packed crowd – are honored with a bronze plaque at the corner of the Haley lot.

La Jeste Clown College

89 Cardinal Avenue, at Park Row (1-467 555 0133, www.lajeste.got). El Train B, C, D, E to Amusement Mile Station. **Map** p29 D2 ㉙

This European-style school for circus performers teaches classes in mime, clowning, juggling, and other specialty arts. La Jeste offers children's programs as well as workshops for adults on improv and prop comedy.

Orpheum Theater

1220 W 15th Street, W of Cardinal Avenue (1-465 555 0130, www.orpheum theater.got). El Train B, D to W 20th Street Station.

The most expansive of Midtown's popular Theater Row venues, the Orpheum holds 1,900, with steep discounts on seats in the balcony and upper balcony. Behind-the-scenes technical wizardry makes it the ideal venue for watching extravagant spectaculars such as the submerged stage of *Atlantica* and the pyrotechnics of *The Mad Monk*.

Rosemont Theater

Second Avenue, at W 15th Street (1-465 555 0140, www.rosemont.got). El Train C, E, Q to Robinson Station.

Having recently celebrated its 75th birthday, the historic Rosemont still fills its seats three shows a day (except Sundays). Almost every notable local thespian has trod the boards here, and the venue is rumoured to be haunted by anywhere from six to a dozen distinct spectres. Student groups and seniors are sometimes admitted for free.

La Scala Theater

80 Second Avenue, at Park Row (1-465 555 0190, www.lascalatheater.got).

El Train C, D, E to Park Row Station.
Map p28 C2 **30**

For decades, plywood shuttered the windows of La Scala, but Park Row's resurgent fortunes have brought new life to this art deco movie house, which opened in 1933. Foreign films and stage productions by Gotham State U drama students now fill the bill.

Sports teams

Basketball: Gotham Guardsmen
Corner of E Merchant Street & First Avenue (1-465 555 0102, www. gothamguardsmen.got). El Train B, C, D, E to Cornerstone Station.

The Guardsmen hold court in the 15,000-seat Midtown Arena, frequently playing to a full house of fans despite the team's multi-season playoff drought. Rising star Kazik Dell, a dunk-happy crowd-pleaser, often remains courtside after the game to sign autographs and pose for pictures.

College football: Gotham State University Wildcats
1180 Tolson Street, on the GSU campus (1-465 555 0124, www.gsuwildcats.got). El Train B, C, D, E, G, Q to Kingston Square Station.

Gotham Guardsmen

On crisp fall Saturdays during college football season, GSU alums drift into town for campus tailgating. If you can't score tickets to the game, nearby bars offer the next best thing with televised big-screen action and an elbow-to-elbow crush of enthusiastic fans.

Football: Gotham Goliaths
3542 South Fisk Way, Somerset (1-467 555 0127, www.gotham goliaths.got).

Tickets go fast for the Gotham Goliaths, especially for their grudge matchup with the rival Metropolis Monarchs. Despite their name and a reputation for punishing, full-contact play, the Goliaths are usually cast as the underdog, making a victory a cause for city-wide celebrations. The open-air environs of Powers Stadium often mean the possibility of rain or snow.

Hockey: Gotham Blades
556 East Solomon Street, at Lansing Avenue (1-467 555 0198, www.gotham blades.got). El Train Q to Solomon Street Station.

Hockey in Gotham draws smaller crowds than football or basketball, but Blades fans are a diehard bunch. Blades Arena is located in the suburb of Bristol. Its lobby displays interactive exhibits and memorabilia from the team's five national championships.

Theater Row
Blocks near W 15th Street (1-465 555 0174, www.gothamtheaterrow.got). El Train C, E, Q to Robinson Station.

Traditionally, it's the Midtown theaters along Chester Street and Cardinal Avenue that welcome the biggest of the big-ticket shows. The area's Theater Row designation is well earned, thanks to fresh lineups of crowd-pleasing musicals and dramas showcasing nationally known actors and playwrights. Tickets for the hottest performances, including the in-demand seats at the Orpheum and the Rosemont, can be purchased on a standby basis at a hefty discount. Visit the Official Gotham City Information Center (p62).

DON'T let pickpockets ruin your vacation.

Gotham City is home to some of the world's most prolific criminals, so make sure your valuables are protected at all times.

YOUR SAFETY IS OUR PRIORITY.

MAYOR
OF GOTHAM

Essentials

Powers Hotel p58

Hotels

Gotham City has more hotel choices than ever, with new construction and renovation projects that have brought long-shuttered locations back to their former glory. Old Gotham is all about nostalgic grandeur, while the Bowery and Little Odessa have seen the arrival of the kind of modernized, youth-themed hotels that are popular in London and Sydney. Don't be surprised if you can't book a room in your hotel of choice during Gotham's festivals – though there are plenty of mid- and low-priced spots with vacancies available nearly all year. Many hotels combine guest rooms with entertainment such as piano bars, breweries or casinos.

The venues listed in this chapter have been designated a price band to give you an idea of what you can expect to pay, but note that rates can vary wildly according to the season or room category. As a general guide, expect to pay $500 or more per night for a double room in the **Deluxe** category, $300-$500 for **Expensive** hotels, $150-$300 for **Moderate** properties and under $150 for **Budget** lodgings. And don't forget to factor in Gotham's 13% hotel tax.

Deluxe

Orchard Hotel

665 Earl Street, at Cornerstone Court (1-465 555 0168, www.orchard.got). El Train B, C, D, E to Cornerstone Station. The sweeping arches rising above the marble-floored lobby are just some of the architectural flourishes that set the Orchard Hotel apart. A fixture of Old Gotham since 1893, the Orchard was a favorite of U.S. presidents and foreign heads of state throughout the 20th century. Old-fashioned elegance is evident in its uniformed bellhops and silver-framed bathroom mirrors.

ESSENTIALS

Hyde Towers

Powers Hotel

*W 10th Street, at Cardinal Avenue
(1-465 555 0199, www.powershotel.got).
El Train A, B, C to W 10th Street Station.*
Built by Gotham's super-rich Powers
family in the 1950s, this Upper East
Side landmark is currently operated by
Maria Powers as a hotel and art gallery.
Every room is decorated in the style of
a different local artist, while the upper-
story lounge and observation deck
(complete with pool) are showcases
for rare pieces from the Powers art
collection.

Expensive

Harborgate Towers

*320 Horace Avenue (1-467 555 0153,
www.harborgatetowers.got). El Train
C, D to Jeremiah Avenue Station.*
This Midtown housing project received
a gentrification facelift in the late
'90s. Its upper floors tend to be home
to young professionals who throw
frequent, noisy, balcony parties. If
that sounds like your crowd, consider
booking one of the rental units on the
lowest three floors (minimum booking
one week). Most guests share the cost
of a unit with multiple friends – room
capacity is capped at ten. Harborgate is
booked months in advance during the
summer festival season.

Hotel Aventine

*Second Avenue, at W 1st Street (1-465
555 0142, www.hotelaventine.got).
El Train C, E, G to Coventry Station.*
The Aventine casino-hotel is a reason-
ably priced option near the Bowery.
Most of the hotel's bookings come from
local gamblers enjoying an extended
night out. The Aventine is unique in its
focus on kid-friendly attractions, offering an arcade and a multi-story play
area where children can be dropped off
under the supervision of hotel staff.

Hyde Towers

*Earl Street, at Cornerstone Court
(1-465 555 0125, www.hydetowers.got).
El Train A, B, C, D to City Hall Station.*
This unassuming brick edifice in
Chelsea hides a wonderfully luxurious
hotel equipped with 24/7 door staff and

discreet security cams for shielding the privacy of its tenants from onlookers. A favorite spot for celebs and sports stars visiting Gotham, Hyde Towers has a first-rate spa and a professional-quality weight room.

Moderate

Gotham City Arms Hotel

W 1st Street, at First Avenue (1-465 555 0189, www.gothamcityarmshotel.got). El Train C, E, G to Coventry Station.
This swanky spot in the Bowery district is a riot of carefully clashing fabrics, tiles and wall hangings – all part of new owner P Dekker's avant-garde vision for an interactive, mentally challenging 3D experience. Downstairs, the Hallucination Lounge serves up chilled cocktails, and the swimming pool is stocked with goldfish.

HMS Tar

Pier 5, at the end of Kelly Street (1-465 555 0172, www.hmstar.got). El Train C, D, E to Harbor Street Station.

ORCHARD HOTEL

Orchard Hotel p57

This mid-century ocean steamer is no longer seaworthy and is now permanently moored near Port Adams. The snug cabins (112 in all) offer comfortable beds and washrooms, and a view of the sights through tiny portholes. There's an outdoor deck pool too.

Hotel Parvenu

440 Francis Street, at Clay Street (1-467 555 0168, www.hotelparvenu.got). El Train B, D, G to Caruana Station.
Featuring unfinished wooden planks, bare brick walls and striking light fittings, this former sardine cannery provides an airy, modern take on urban minimalism. Free Wi-Fi and countless gadget-charging outlets make it a favorite of young professionals.

Budget

Excelsior Motel

N Cumberland Street, at Foote Street (1-467 555 0178, www.excelsiormotel. got). El Train B, C, D, E to Amusement Mile Station.
One of the last relics from the glory days of the now-decaying Amusement Mile, the Excelsior Motel has weathered the area's downturn and is poised to benefit from its underground art resurgence. This no-frills space isn't much to look at, but it can be a cheap place to catch some Zs while planning strategic day-trips to some of Gotham's pricey hotspots.

Harbor Light Motor Lodge

7789 8th Street, at Robertson Way (1-467 555 0114, www.harborlight motorlodge.got). El Train E to Little Odessa Station.
Just by the Kane Bridge off-ramp before entering Little Odessa, the Harbor Light Motor Lodge is an affordable alternative to Gotham's flashier accommodations while still being within the city itself. Simple, clean rooms open on to the waterfront. The El Train station, one block away, offers full access to Gotham's highlights.

ESSENTIALS

Getting Around

Arriving and leaving

By air

Archie Goodwin International Airport

1-467 555 0156,
www.goodwininternational.got.

The El Train is the cheapest option, but it's not always the fastest. Gotham Airlink ($6, www.gotham airlink.got) connects to the Q train at Robinson Station and the B and C trains at Thornton Station. Shuttle buses (1-467 555 0180, www.gotham transport.got, one way $20, round trip $35, every 30 minutes 5am to 11.30pm daily) make regular stops in Midtown, Old Gotham, the Bowery, and Park Row. Because Turkish Airlines has recently opened up a high-profile new route to Gotham, passengers get 50% off upon presentation of their boarding pass. A Gotham taxi often charges a flat fare of $50 plus bridge tolls and tip.

Empire International Airport

1-465 555 0143,
www.empireinternational.got.

Bus routes are the most reliable low-cost way to get to and from Empire International. The 2077 and 5660 buses ($5 one way) can be picked up at the transit station between Park Street and 14th Street; the journey takes 45-60 minutes. A private car or taxi costs about $70 plus tolls and tip.

Public transport

El Train

Gotham's **El Train** network has been in operation for nearly a

century. The noise, the crowded cars, and the confusing tangle of elevated tracks are stubborn sources of pride for locals who have resisted efforts to modernize the system after the style of Metropolis' maglev monorails.

Stations are usually named for the street on which they're located, or the nearest landmark. Trains are identified by colors and numbers, but picking them out and determining whether a given train is running an express or a local route is famously difficult. You can pick up free route maps at many hotels, gift shops, or eateries. Poster-sized maps are on display at every station, but are not guaranteed to be up to date.

Stranded bunches of tourists are common at El Train stations. The El runs 24/7, but many stations lack late-night security. Travel in groups. During extended waits, remain within the range of the station's overhead lighting and stay far away from shadows and dark corners.

Fares & tickets

You'll need to buy an **ElCard** to travel on the El Train network. Cards are available at tourist kiosks, many hotel concierge desks and at automated payment machines in the stations themselves. Base fare for a single ride is $2.75, and one ElCard can be used by up to four people. A **HyperElCard** allows unlimited rides within two timing windows: a seven-day pass ($30) and a 30-day pass ($110).

Boat

The **Gotham River Ferry Authority** (GRFA, 1-467 555 0188, www.grfa.got) runs the over-the-water routes connecting Gotham

City with Metropolis. The **Tricorner Passenger Ferry** ($5 one way, $12 day pass), popular with commuters, is accessible via Tricorner Yards Station on El Train routes A, B, C, and E. The **Port Adams Dock Ferry** can be reached via the Harbor Street Station on El Train routes C, D, and E and offers both passenger and vehicular transport ($7-$25 one way). Visit the website for schedules.

Bus

Buses are generally not recommended for travel within the city itself. Stops are limited and the routes are susceptible to traffic delays and vehicle breakdowns. All buses can be boarded at the transit station between Park Street and 14th Street (14th Street Station on El Train routes A, B, C, and E), which is home to **Gotham Metro Transit** (GMT, 1-465 555 01262, www.gothammetrotransit.got) and is the hub for all routes connecting Gotham with its outlying suburbs. Ticket discounts are available for seniors and students. Check the website for offers and updated schedules.

Rail

Gotham's passenger rail system is a separate entity from its in-city El Train network. The **Wayne Yards Terminal** (1-465 555 0183, www.wayneyardsterminal.got) is accessible via the A, B, D, and Q lines on the El Train. From there, rail lines lead out to the Gotham suburbs and more than 100 points upstate.

Taxis

Feel free to flag down a Gotham cab if its rooflight is illuminated – the sign that it's unoccupied and its driver is on the clock. Be sure to only patronize licensed cabs. The GCPD

recommends ignoring any vehicle with an odd or suspicious appearance – such as clown colors or a top-hatted theme – as these are the calling cards of some of the city's more flamboyant criminals.

Cabs can carry up to four passengers. Pricing starts at $3, plus $0.50 per fifth of a mile or per minute idling, with a $1 surcharge during rush hour (4-8pm Mon-Fri). The average fare for a three-mile ride is $16, but this will vary depending on the time and traffic. Always ask for a receipt, which contains the driver's number and meter number in case of complaints.

For assistance or to locate lost items, call the **Gotham Taxi Commission** (1-465 555 0104, www.gctaxicommission.got).

Driving

Car hire is cheaper in the suburbs. Be advised that parking in Gotham is infamously difficult and laden with regulations and special exceptions. Read all parking signs and make a note of numbers to call if your vehicle is towed or impounded.

Cycling

Gotham's **MetroBike** system (www.gothammetrobike.got) allows access to bikes at 250 docking stations across the city. Prices are $10 for 24 hours, $25 for seven days.

Walking

Gotham's grid pattern of streets makes navigation relatively easy, except in parts of Old Gotham where the higgledy-piggledy layout means it's easy to get confused. Plenty of outfits offer walking tours, such as the Gotham Historical Society (www.gothamhistoricalsociety.got) and the sensationalist Gotham True Crime (www.gothamtruecrime.got).

ESSENTIALS

Resources A-Z

Accident & emergency

In an emergency, dial **911** for an ambulance, police, or the fire department. The following hospitals have emergency rooms:

Gotham City General Hospital *2233 Barday Street (1-467 555 0123). El Train A, B, C, E to Mercy Station.*
North Central Hospital *554 W 5th Street (1-467 555 0142). El Train A, B, C, D, E to Wayne Tower Station.*
Wayne Medical Center *200 Summit Lane (1-465 555 0131). El Train B, C, D, E to Cornerstone Station.*

Internet

Gotham City Public Library *1-465 555 0155, www.gcpubliclibrary.got.*
All branches of the City Public Library offer free online access and computers for public use. Computers have a time limit of 45 minutes per user per day.
Gotham City Wireless
www.gothamcitywireless.got.
This utility has installed hotspots all around Gotham to provide free public wireless access. Coverage is at its strongest in Midtown and South Gotham. Visit the website for more information and a map of Wi-Fi nodes.
Jitters *1-467 555 0106, www.jittersgotham.got.*
Most branches of this popular coffee chain (p39) offer free Wi-Fi; search the website for your nearest location.

Police

The Gotham City Police Department (GCPD) has stations all over the city, with a heavier presence in the touristy areas around Midtown and Old Gotham. If you're lucky, you might see GCPD operate their so-called bat signal, in the hope of attracting the attention of The Batman. To find the nearest police precinct or for information about GCPD services, call 1-465 555 0150 or visit www.gcpd.got.

Safety

Gotham's crime rate has dropped in recent years, largely due (or so some claim) to the efforts of the masked vigilante known as The Batman. Still, parts of the city, notably Park Row, the Bowery and the Warehouse District, are best avoided after dark. Don't flaunt your valuables, keep away from poorly lit or deserted streets, and be alert for pickpockets.

Time

Gotham City is on Eastern Standard Time, which is five hours behind Greenwich Mean Time. Clocks are set forward one hour in early March for Daylight Saving Time (Eastern Daylight Time) and back one hour at the beginning of November.

Tipping

In restaurants, it is customary to tip at least 15%.

Tourist information

Official Gotham City Information Center at Theater Row *6200 Chester Street, at Cardinal Avenue (1-465 555 0177, www.gogotham.got). El Train B, D to W 20th Street Station.* **Open** 9am-7pm Mon-Fri; 10am-7pm Sat; 11am-7pm Sun.
The main tourist office provides free maps and can book accommodation.

Legend of The Batman

Mystery surrounds Gotham's most famous citizen.

Gothamites swear by the existence of their hometown protector, despite scepticism still lobbed in their direction after nearly 20 years of Bat-sightings. The fact that the costumed vigilante dubbed 'The Batman' has never stepped forward to cash in on his fame has led many outsiders to dismiss him as an urban legend, or a wildly exaggerated story cooked up by a sensationalist press.

If you share similar sentiments, it's best to keep them to yourself: disbelief in The Batman is a sure-fire mark of a Gotham outsider. Instead, chat up the locals at a tavern in the Warehouse District or a dive bar on Park Row. Most people are happy to share their tales of close encounters with The Batman, and after hearing a half-dozen of them you'll probably start craning your neck toward the night sky hoping to catch your own glimpse of The Bat.

Here's what to look for, compiled from years of eyewitness reports.

Gadgets

Unlike Metropolis' latest hero, The Batman doesn't appear to have any superhuman powers. But that doesn't mean he's ordinary. Using a retractable cable gun, he traverses the city from rooftop to rooftop, leaving behind telltale claw marks in many of Gotham's taller buildings. He swoops down into alleyways, interrupting robberies and breaking up beatings. Sharpened metal projectiles shaped like a bat's silhouette are thrown at enemies, and several of these have allegedly been recovered from crime scenes and delivered into the hands of private collectors. The so-called 'Batmobile' – a matte-black roadster with the armor of a tank and the engine of a Formula One car – occasionally roars through the near-empty streets after midnight, although it has never been caught on film. Some swear they've also witnessed a supersonic 'Batplane', but such sightings are officially attributed to military flyovers.

Criminals

Street toughs aren't the only criminals said to have been collared by the bat-eared vigilante. Since The Batman launched his nocturnal crusade, criminals with an equally theatrical bent have become media sensations. Thanks to The Batman's intervention, their high-profile capers have ended in arrest by the GCPD and incarceration in the Arkham Asylum for the Criminally Insane. The sadistic Joker is the most notorious of these rogues. Close behind him are twisted figures the public has dubbed Deadshot, Killer Croc, Harley Quinn, and more.

Identity

Who is The Batman? In light of the crimefighter's access to advanced technology, many have speculated that he is a foot soldier bankrolled by the wealthy and powerful – with Wayne Enterprises and the U.S. government two common string-pullers in the minds of conspiracy theorists. Given The Batman's nearly 20-year career, it's entirely possible that his costume has been passed down and worn by a succession of different Batmen.

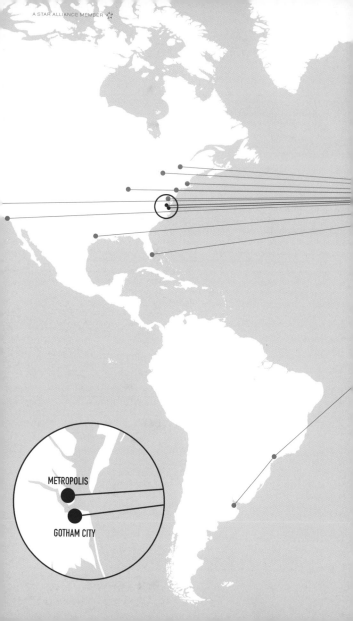

METROPOLIS

GOTHAM CITY

Don't Miss

Daily Planet Building p33

WHAT'S BEST

A City of Heroes

Metropolis is famous for its forward-looking, optimistic spirit, captured in its nickname 'City of Tomorrow'. With wide avenues lined with gleaming skyscrapers, and an entrepreneurial spirit that derives from its long-standing tech industry, it has an infectious energy that inspires visitors. While neighbouring Gotham City can seem insular, Metropolis welcomes you with open arms.

The city, of course, is still emerging from the devastation of the recent Kryptonian attack, but Metropolis has made great strides thanks to hard work and corporate investment. A notable contributor to the city's rebuilding is **LexCorp** (box p45), which is blazing new trails into uncharted fields of science for the betterment of humankind – according to its press releases, at

least. No one can visit Metropolis and not acknowledge the attack, but most locals prefer to talk about the rebuilding, or to point in the direction of Heroes Park (formerly known as Centennial Park) where a grassy expanse covers the scars left by the gravity weapon. A statue of the astonishing champion who emerged on that day also stands in the park. Now dubbed **Superman** (box p63), this figure has adopted Metropolis as his own when he isn't rescuing victims from floods or preventing oil tanker explosions all around the world.

City neighbourhoods

Metropolis grew out of the colonial outpost of Fort Hob, leveraging its position on the Atlantic to become a destination for immigrants. Many of those newcomers used their

ingenuity to benefit their adopted city in the fields of science and technology. Today's Metropolis is still a place of wonder, as seen in the city's advanced maglev Monorail network. Bridges connect the central island of New Troy to the other boroughs, while ferries link Metropolis to Gotham City.

The central island of **New Troy** is often the first thing that comes to mind when people think about Metropolis, but the entire city encompasses the boroughs of Queensland Park, Park Ridge, and Bakerline. Bordered on one side by the West River and on the other by Hob's River, New Troy itself contains **Midtown** and **Metro Square**, as well as the **Financial District**. Notable concentrations of culture and commerce include the **Arts District**, the **Fashion District** and the **Jewelry District**. Income levels and ethnicity may vary across New Troy, but its inhabitants share an obvious pride in their hometown.

On the east side of New Troy sits **Hob's Bay**, once home to 19th-century tenements but now a trendy area that trades on its working-class reputation. Though some areas near Hob's Bay developed the unfortunate moniker 'Suicide Slum', the neighborhood has undergone a transformation at the hands of LexCorp's 'Simon Project', providing refurbished low-income housing. **Chinatown** is near Hob's River, as is the cozy collegiate site of **Metropolis University**.

Queensland Park lies along the West River and its subdivisions include Newtown, Mount Royal, Pelham, North Bridge, and Old City. Along the waterfront you'll find public and private beaches and exclusive estates amid corporate glass-and-steel mid-rises that house communications companies.

Newtown is home to several of the city's smaller museums and is

experiencing a housing boom, with an influx of young moneyed professionals who have renovated the area's ageing brownstones. In **Mount Royal**, thousands of students attend two more educational establishments, the Metro University of Art and the Metropolis Institute of Technology. The **Old City**, named for the very first settlement in the area, is the site of the North Street Seaport, while **Pelham** is a burgeoning arts community.

Bakerline has traditionally been home to Metropolis' middle-class white-collar drones, but changing demographics have brought in a twentysomething techie crowd employed by LexCorp and smaller competitors. Old-money estates occupy the southern seaboard, while the neighborhood of **Oaktown** is still an immigrant-friendly enclave. Berkowitz Airport is located on the fringes of Bakerline.

Park Ridge encompasses the neighborhoods of Racine and Vernon, and is one of the wealthiest and most historic parts of Metropolis. **Racine** is an upscale artistic haven; you can dine at the exclusive LeMarvin Bistro (p41), for example, or stroll the narrow streets beneath a spreading canopy of oak branches. **Vernon**, largely composed of single-family homes, is located on the way to Metropolis International Airport.

Buildings of note

In a city with a history as long as that of Metropolis, the eras can be read in the lines of its buildings. Visit **City Hall** (p32) for one of the oldest and greatest architectural treasures in Metropolis and to tour its breathtaking Beaux-Arts interior, dating from the late 19th century. Turn-of-the-20th-century splendor is on display at the **Schaffenberger** gallery (p53), as well as in the heart

Temples to science

Metropolis is famous for its focus on science and education. Accordingly, its museums are among the best in the world.

The **Metropolis History Museum** (p35) sits in Hob's Bay and offers a back-in-time journey through the events that shaped the city. At the **Metropolis Museum of Art** (p36), priceless pieces from the Great Masters hang on the walls, while its temporary shows are often one of the city's hottest tickets. The **Julian Gallery** (p35) honors the maritime history of the Atlantic seaboard, with an 18th-century shipwrecked galleon on display amid artefacts allegedly gathered from the lost civilization of Atlantis. For children, the **Metropolis Science Exploratorium** (p36) in Queensland Park is a favorite, with walk-through re-creations of the city's history and 3D movie screenings. Those who like a little nostalgia with their futurism won't want to miss the **Jules Verne Extra-Terrestrial Museum** (p35) in Bakerline, where a steampunk-

of the Jewelry District at the **Digby & Sons** (p43) and **Schwarzenoff** (p44) stores. The grand and venerable department store Mr **Leonards** (p43) draws crowds to the Fashion District, while the **Metropolis Grand Hotel** (p38) features a cathedral-like ambiance with its multi-story stained-glass windows.

Art deco had a major influence on Metropolis from the 1920s through the '40s, and there's no better example than the clock-faced **Hammersmith Tower** (p34), which was the tallest building in the city for decades. The **Daily Planet Building** (p33) is a notable example of post-war modernism, with its neat parallel lines and abhorrence of filigree – though the stylized bronze globe in its lobby is iconic enough to pop up on postcards.

Among the city's modern standouts are the wave-like glass cylinder of Hob's Bay's **Atwater Tower** (p38) and the triumphant spire of **LexCorp Tower** (p33), which is open to the public.

Metropolis History Museum p35

Metropolis Park p36

Sights & Museums

DON'T MISS

Metropolis Park (p36) isn't huge, but it packs a boating reservoir, a public garden, and a network of jogging trails into a wooded space at the corner of Bloomsbury Street and Fifth Avenue. Follow the Avenue of Tomorrow down to Wardenclyffe Street and you'll find yourself at **Metro Square** (p35), a neon nexus of blinking lights and souvenir stands that reaches maximum hype every New Year's Eve. On the Lower East Side, **Glenmorgan Square** (p33) faces the waterfront and is perfect for catching rays while enjoying an impromptu food-cart picnic.

And many thousands of visitors come to Metropolis for no other purpose than to visit **Heroes Park** (p34), the newly dedicated open-air memorial commemorating those who lost their lives on the day of the Kryptonian attack. Heroes Park is a place of remembrance and reflection, and a celebration of the resilience of the citizens who are proud to call Metropolis their home.

infused voyage into the changing visions of tomorrow is presented through the lens of popular sci-fi. You can get your fill of Metropolis' leading export – high-tech optimism – at the **Avenue of Tomorrow** (p32), the multi-block Midtown showcase for consumer electronics and experimental products that has also housed generations of cutting-edge launches. **LexCorp Plaza** is a new addition to the scene, constructed in the aftermath of the Kryptonian attack and anchored by LexCorp Tower. Company employees mix with tourists and gawkers, sometimes demonstrating drones and robots temporarily freed from their high-security laboratories.

Spaces for all

Metropolis is a city that celebrates its citizens, and many areas have been set aside for festivals and community gatherings – check the **Calendar** (pp24-27) for the can't-miss events. On quieter days, these spots are a fine place to relax and take a breather.

BESSOLO

BISTRO

SPECTACULAR OCEAN VIEW

OPEN 7 DAYS A WEEK
FROM 10AM – MIDNIGHT
FRI & SAT UNTIL 1AM

22 WATERFRONT STREET
TEL: 1 - 637 555 0138

DON'T MISS THE "BESS" MEATLOAF

Chez Joey's p38

WHAT'S BEST

Tasting Notes

The people of Metropolis love to eat out. As a city built on an open immigration policy, with a vibrant melting-pot culture, it's no surprise that Metropolis boasts a diverse culinary scene that's not afraid to experiment. In some cases this can be eye-openingly literal – LexCorp operates a food-science lab and has been known to introduce sugar substitutes and fat-burning starches developed in its test kitchens to surprised diners. Visit as many neighbourhoods as you can, to experience both the heritage of the city's inhabitants and taste the zest of optimism that seems to season everything coming out of Metropolis.

To the hilt

In a bleeding-edge city like Metropolis, expect nothing less than cooking as a science. The city is home to dozens of restaurants specialising

in molecular gastronomy, with **LeMarvin Bistro** (p41) as the poster child for the movement. Gawkers come for the celebrity sightings, but the wait-times are equally jaw-dropping, unless you've reserved several months in advance. Seating is a little easier at **Chez Joey's** (p38), a haven for New American fare with Japanese accents. Enjoy the pumpkin toast with miso and goat cheese, and the curried lobster roll on a stylish black bun, but don't forget your formal wear. The city's highest-rated Italian eatery is **Carlini's** (p38), featuring traditional dishes from Sicily to Sardinia, plus a take-out bakery. Not all of the city's five-star restaurants are in New Troy or Park Ridge, so plan on exploring the upper-crust avenues of Bakerline or Queensland Park to truly indulge in the VIP lifestyle.

Dooley's Pub p39

No-frills thrills

There are plenty of upscale dining options in Metropolis, but this unpretentious city offers its widest array of choices to the casual diner and families. Particularly during the reconstruction, many locals returned to the simple comforts of a good burger and a cold beer. Basic menus providing deceptively delicious fare are handed out at booths and diner counters across the city, with a special concentration in Hob's Bay, Queensland Park, Bakerline, and the docks along the West River.

Dooley's Pub (p39), conveniently located next door to the Daily Planet Building, is perhaps the quintessential example of the no-frills style, having set the benchmark for soups, sandwiches and burgers for more than 50 years. Don't leave the city without trying

its famous grilled fish sliders.

No matter where you are in Metropolis, you're sure to find a **Big Belly Burger** (p38). The national chain has put down roots in numerous cities, but the custom menu in Metropolis is packed with unique choices not offered elsewhere, such as the double-patty Planet Special. Then there's **Uri's Family Restaurant** (p41), a franchised chain restaurant whose original location is a down-to-earth diner on Mundell Street. Many items on the original Uri's menu have remained unchanged since it opened, including

In the un-gentrified corners of Hob's Bay, the **Ace O'Clubs** (p37) tavern still holds a pickle spear on the side. In the court, serving up pub fare for generations of hungry dockworkers. a Metropolis-style hot dog – an all-beef dog topped with sweet chili, spicy mustard, diced onions and

Bessolo Bistro p38

DON'T MISS

Eating & Drinking

Hop-heads will want to pay a visit to **Koul-Brau Breweries (p41)** to dine on wood-fired pizza at the brewpub after touring the working brewery and bottler. Or stop by **Karl's Pump & Brew (p41)** on a Friday or Saturday night, to take in the live musical entertainment in a space that once housed an auto repair shop. Indulge your nose by following the salty tang wafting from **Evans Pretzel Factory (p33)**, which recently celebrated its 75th anniversary and is still going strong. Need a caffeine injection to keep going after all that snacking? **Mo's Café (p41)** serves up a wonderful cold brew infused with mulling spices and an aioli breakfast sandwich worthy of a postcard.

Up for adventure

Metropolis is the perfect place to experience globe-trotting cuisine. Indian, Asian, South American, Australian and varied European cuisines provide plenty of options, sometimes sharing space on the same menu – or even inside the same dish. For avant-garde fusion cuisine, look no further than **Chaney's (p38)** in Hob's Bay, where visionary chef Carmen Chaney cooks with liquid nitrogen on an ever-changing tasting menu. In Chinatown, seek out **Dynasty (p39)** for a pan-Asian experience that unites five kitchens with specialties from China, Japan, Vietnam, Thailand and Korea. Or you can venture south of the equator at **Carrasco's (p38)**, a locals-only Chilean spot with a long wine list and life-affirming empanadas.

Even seemingly straightforward Metropolis eateries can provide an unexpected – and delicious – twist to their dishes. At the **Alewife (p37)** near the Queensland Docks, seafood from the cold waters of the Atlantic is used to create a full-bodied, spicy bouillabaisse, with tasty morsels of lobster, oysters, mussels, cod, mackerel, crab and shrimp. Or hit **Bessolo Bistro (p38)** on the very tip of New Troy island, an inviting hangout where sweet, salty and savory flavors are combined in classic fillers such as meatloaf and pot pie.

Fashion District

Unique Selling Points

WHAT'S BEST

There are few cities in the United States as retail-centric as Metropolis, where even the vital high-tech industry is largely reliant on sales of consumer electronics to keep it afloat. Many gadgets – just out of beta testing – are sold only on the **Avenue of Tomorrow** (p32) or in the LexCorp store on Tesla Avenue.

The city's Jewelry District, anchored by **Digby & Sons** (p43) and **Schwartzenoff** (p44), attracts well-heeled shoppers and wishful gawkers alike. The adjacent Fashion District is home to legendary department store **Mr Leonards** (p43) and also secondary quarters filled with themed shops, namely the shoe district, the garment district and the fur district.

On the campus of Metropolis University you can purchase official University gear from the same stores as students (minus the discount, of course). Sweatshirts, ball caps and other Met U wear are also available at **Empire Pier** (p43), a family-friendly mini-mall that extends into Hob's River.

Don't forget the city's museum scene when writing up your shopping list. The **Metropolis History Museum** (p35) has a multi-story gift shop overlooking Hob's River that sells educational toys and books by local historians. You can buy prints and posters of your favorite masterpieces at the **Metropolis Museum of Art** (p36), while the nautical environs of the **Julian Gallery** (p35) are where you'll find genuine shipwreck artefacts for sale, from pirate-hauled golden doubloons to the nails that once held together a Greek trireme.

Schott's Toys p43

Shopping

Grab your gifts

Want to remember your visit with a keepsake, or need to stock up on goodies for friends and family back home? Metropolis has got you covered. There are gift shops on nearly every corner, including dozens in **Metro Square** (p35) alone. Locals usually give these outfits a wide berth, but one that attracts a steady stream of neighbourhood business is **Metro Souvenirs** (p43) at Second Avenue, thanks to its three-level layout showcasing unique pieces by local crafters and artisans. Customised gizmos are par for the course at **Schott's Toys** (p43), where modern software has been retrofitted by hand into traditional designs to come up with marching tin soldiers and teddy bears that speak 23 languages. The comic book adventures dreamed up at the offices above **Blaze Comics** (p43) are still hooking new readers, and their retail business reportedly received a boost after the real-world emergence of a certain 'Man of Steel'. Speaking of Superman, the best place to get S-shield merchandise is at **Heroes Park** (p44). Many of the souvenirs for sale are of dubious quality – or in questionable taste – but you can't beat the selection or the price.

Seeking out sales

The Fashion District is an irresistible lure for those who want to refresh their wardrobes, but its high-end designer boutiques are too pricey for most wallets. That's where bargain hunting comes in, and the locals have a host of tips and tricks for scoring a steal.

Post-season sales usually start just after Christmas and last through mid January, with a second sales season hitting Memorial Day weekend in late May and carrying through mid June. During these times, Mr Leonards and other stores in the Fashion District roll out discount racks and uncover sale tables to attract sharp-eyed fashion foragers. Check the ads in the *Daily Planet* for late-breaking bargains, or try the outlet malls in Metropolis distant ring of suburbs.

At **Mary Alice's Consignment Shop** (p43), the bargains are available year-round, with new pieces unveiled first thing in the morning (and often gone by noon). Hit the flea markets in Hob's Bay every Saturday and Sunday morning from 6am to noon: you'll find great deals on vintage clothing, antique furnishings, and handmade artworks, with buyers encouraged to haggle over the final price.

METROPOLIS'
KNOCK OUT
SPOT

THE ACE O' CLUBS

HAPPY HOUR
From 7 PM
EVERY NIGHT

11 TURF STREET, HOB'S BAY STATION.
OPEN UNTIL 4AM MONDAY TO SATURDAY.

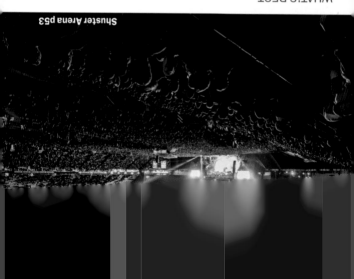
Shuster Arena p53

Face the Music

Metropolis keeps on buzzing after the sun goes down. In a city famous for its music scene, you'll often find performance venues are packed and small-stage dive bars are standing room only. But live performance isn't the only way to experience music in Metropolis, not with a string of high-energy dance clubs electrifying the East Side.

Metropolis is a see-and-be-seen city, and its residents know it – don't be surprised when celebrities and paparazzi show up at a club, and don't get discouraged when that makes it even harder for regular people to make it past the bouncers and inside the velvet rope.

No matter what kind of entertainment you're looking for, the communal energy of millions of people is an invigorating high. You can feel it for yourself in participatory spaces such as **Sienna Hall** (p48), a venue for professional comedians and improv troupes that also hosts open-mic sessions that encourage audience participation. Meanwhile, lounge-bar decadence is on offer at the **Border Room** (p46), where low-key piano and drum noodlings soon turn into multi-instrument jams as guests show off their chops.

Superstar headliners regularly fill the stands at Shuster Arena, but there are plenty of places where you can get up close and personal with the performers – especially the hotspots to the north-east of the Metropolis University campus. The city's small-business community encourages entrepreneurism, so every time you visit you're sure to find a fresh crop of hopeful venues with something unique to offer.

String Theory p49

Musical highs

Live music is the city's heart and soul. Every inhabitant seems to have a performing gene, and it doesn't take long for even the most reserved visitors to get into the spirit. A typical tavern in Metropolis will have a barstool and microphone off in a corner with several musical instruments at hand – it's expected that a succession of guests will take turns, initiating singalongs and kicking off jam sessions. A similar spirit infuses the city's dedicated music temples too, from the mega-stadium vibe of Shuster Arena to the big but approachable environs of **Siegel Music Hall** (p48). Due to the hall's optimal acoustics, many national touring acts have recorded live albums while performing at Siegel. Musical acts with more modest ambitions will find a welcoming environment in the blocks surrounding Metropolis University. In particular, the **Longshore Ballroom** (p47) is a favorite of indie rock acts who have yet to make the jump into the mainstream. You'll encounter a lot of history in **Lucy's Pub** (p47), once you look past the grimy surroundings and recognize the scuffed stage that helped birth the punk scene in the late 1970s. For jazz, there's no better experience than the **Metropolitan Club** (p48), where

venues have helped make Reddick Street an indisputable EDM mecca, but the more intimate, chilled-out environment of Supernova will at least allow you to hold a conversation without shouting.

Met U is determined to grow its own strain of club culture, with **String Theory** (p49) a breakout hit. Tobias Whale's **El Cielo** (p46) cultivates a different feel, with old-world decor complementing the throbbing pulse of electronica.

Dance all night

Nova (p48) regularly hosts EDM celebrities like Leslie Willis (aka Livewire). The celebrated club opened in 1975 and helped set the tone for popular culture. It remains as busy as ever, which is what prompted the creation of its little sister, **Supernova** (p49). Both

More casinos are coming to Metropolis thanks to recent changes in zoning laws, but for now the sector is dominated by Tony Gallo's **Utopia Casino** (p49). With private rooms for high-rollers and endless rows of slot machines for penny-players, the Utopia is one of the few Metropolis nightspots that never closes. Performance stages and buffet dinner halls are still packed at 4am.

DON'T MISS

Nightlife

Supernova p49

legends have performed every weekend since the venue opened its doors in 1932.

Expect the unexpected

The reconstruction effort has undeniably revitalised parts of the city, and the spirit of innovation it sparked has even spread to unaffected areas. Renovation has transformed most of the Hob's Bay waterfront and entire blocks of Bakertine, where the **Kenmore Bowling Alley (p47)** has been the beneficiary of a trendy interior makeover that belies its old-fashioned exterior.

Even the urban decay of 'Suicide Slum' is receding as creative entrepreneurs flip the script. Take the **Joy Lounge (p47)** – once an abandoned ex-dressmaking factory, now the cornerstone of a growing bohemian enclave. **The Pit (p48)** has demonstrated similar success, converting an empty warehouse into a crowded club that embraces its neighborhood's reputation for edginess. Another remarkable metamorphosis has occured on the East Side, where a decommissioned Monorail station shook off decades of disuse to become fashionable nightspot the **Rail Line (p48)**.

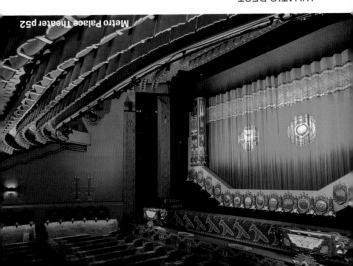
Metro Palace Theater p52

WHAT'S BEST

Dramatic Times

The impact of the Kryptonian attack on the Metropolis cultural scene was huge. Whole swaths of the theater district were erased in an instant, and the construction of replacement venues is so far still in the planning stages. Other cultural hubs survived unscathed, fortunately, and since then they have employed the medium of the arts to help Metropolis work through its emotions of confusion and grief – and to underline the city's renewed sense of determination.

The rebuilding of the city has given new life to neglected gems such as the **Metro Palace Theater** (p52), once an opulent cinematic mecca, now newly restored and updated with state-of-the-art laser projection and a trendy cocktail bar. Out in Queensland Park, the Pelham neighborhood is quickly establishing a reputation for a

thriving underground arts scene. No formal galleries here, but look for converted lofts and repurposed industrial spaces housing artists' communes. A love of Metropolis is a near-universal trait among residents, so plan ahead if you're hoping to get good seats for a game.

Finally, luxurious getaways also await if you know where to look, with the **Apricot Spa** (p51) and similar destinations offering massage and energy therapy to renew both body and spirit.

What a performance

The renowned **Metropolis Ballet** (p52) performs in Minko Hall under the direction of choreographer and artist-in-residence Leonid Stanislavovich. Just a few blocks away is Billups Hall, home to the Metropolis Philharmonic, which

presents broad-appeal concerts every spring featuring musical selections from movie, TV, and video-game soundtracks. At the **Broadrun Jazz Club** (p52), it's all about the music – jazz genres from the innovative to the traditional top the bill inside an intimate venue that is operated in conjunction with the historic Metropolitan Club.

Until the theater district gets back on its feet, the **Greico Theater Workshop** (p52) is doing its best to pick up the slack. The troupe performs at parks and summer festivals while staging interactive workshops at Swinburne Hall. It's this same model that **Awakenings Youth Theater** (p51) aims to follow for grade schoolers through high schoolers, providing creative outlets including acting, playwriting, and costuming.

Theater-lovers should also look out for annual festivals, such as **Grantland Park Outdoor Arts** (p25), which brings drama, music, art exhibitions, food stalls and more to the popular public park.

Gallery gazing

The arts district on Metropolis' West Side is home to dozens of galleries that traffic in artworks ranging from

Metropolis Monarchs p53

the classical to the contemporary. The cornerstone of the area is the **Schaffenberger** (p53), named for shipping tycoon Horace Schaffenberger whose collection of Impressionist masterpieces has attracted crowds since 1899.

The **Simmons Gallery** (p53) offers a more diverse selection of works, and doubles as an auction house for the sale of high-priced artefacts from private collections. The sheer size of the Simmons makes it easy to believe tales that visitors have been lost overnight in its labyrinthine corridors. For the latest on the contemporary art scene, visit the **Turley Gallery** (p53), where multimedia works invite reflection and commentary, often on themes clearly inspired by the recent tragic event.

Fields of dreams

It's fine if you're not a baseball fan, but don't admit it to a local! This is a town that's truly baseball crazy thanks to the **Metropolis Monarchs** (p53), who have won eight World Series titles – fans revere the players as secular icons. The Monarchs play at Schwartz Field in Queensland Park, a historic venue whose narrow aisles and tiny bathrooms are tolerated in the name of tradition, despite a multimillion-dollar cosmetic upgrade.

Many local sports nuts also follow the **Metropolis Mammoths** (p53) at the ice hockey palace of AmerTek Arena. The Arena is a high-tech showcase for the innovations of corporate sponsor AmerTek, but on the ice the Mammoths are all about punishing, old-school physicality. The Mammoths share the Arena with the **Metropolis Metros** basketball team. **Metropolis University college football** (p53) is played inside Shuster Arena, where all 75,000 seats are often filled to capacity.

Calendar

Metropolis Food & Wine Festival

Get prepped for your Metropolis adventure with our pick of the best annual events in the city. Dates and locations can change, so be sure to check websites for up-to-date information before finalizing plans.

Spring

late Apr **Comedy for Charity**
Sienna Hall
www.comedyforcharity.met
Attracting national stand-up stars as well as newcomers trying their luck, this week-long charitable event has pledged its proceeds to benefit the survivors of the recent Kryptonian attack.

late Apr **Cherry Blossom Festival**
West River
www.metropolischerryblossom.met
The beautiful but short-lived bloom of cherry blossoms is the subject of tours,

with traditional music and *Hanami* picnics served up by the city's Japanese community.

early May **Open House Metropolis**
Various venues
www.openhousemetropolis.met
Explore the city from the inside when numerous historic homes and landmarks – including such icons as the Hammersmith Tower and the Daily Planet Building – open their doors to the public, often with guided tours.

mid May **Metropolis Food & Wine Festival**
Hob's River
www.metropolisfoodandwinefest.met
Chefs from around the world descend on Metropolis for three days of all-you-can-taste delights. Tempt your palate and also experiment with new flavors at the open-air stalls on the esplanade.

Metropolis Film Festival

Summer

mid June **Tomorrow Festival**
Avenue of Tomorrow
www.tomorrowfestival.met
This highly anticipated three-day event merges cutting-edge music and technology. Expect free concerts by local bands and demos of the latest products and gadgets as the Avenue of Tomorrow is transformed into a futuristic pedestrian mall.

July-Aug **Minerals of the World**
Queensland Park
www.worldminerals.met
During the summer months, the Metropolis Science Explorarium hosts a traveling exhibition of minerals from around the world, including specimens from Addis Ababa.

4 July **Independence Day Fireworks**
West River waterfront
www.metropolisfireworks.met
Celebrate the American way with a fireworks show above the West River that's as long, loud and spectacular as Washington DC's. Innovations from LexCorp Idea Lab mean that the pyrotechnic flashes sync up with the music broadcast, which is heard throughout the city. The best views are from Queensland Pier, but arrive by 5pm if you don't want to be boxed out.

early Aug **Grantland Park Outdoor Arts**
Grantland Park
www.grantlandparkoutdoorarts.met
During this week-long expo, the grassy lawns of this public park play host to art exhibitors, theater performances, food courts and other entertainment.

late Aug **Bike Metropolis**
Metropolis Park
www.bikemetropolis.met
This 20-mile cycling circuit, in which fitness is more important than speed, passes through some of the city's most scenic neighborhoods.

Autumn

early Oct **Metropolis Film Festival**
Various venues
www.metropolisfilmfest.met
The Metro Palace and dozens of smaller venues host independent and foreign films for the city's cinephiles. Special Monorail routes make it easy to hop between screenings.

mid Oct **Metropolis Marathon**
Heroes Park
www.metropolismarathon.met
Nearly 50,000 runners are expected to cross the finish line in this traditional event. Locals and spectators line the sidewalks, cheering and handing out water and encouragement.

Met U Mega Music

late Oct **Met U Mega Music**
Metropolis University
www.metumegamusic.met
Celebrating the best up-and-comers in indie rock, hip hop and electronica, this weekend festival packs fans into the Longshore Ballroom as well as smaller venues and bars around the campus.

Winter

late Nov **Mr Leonards Thanksgiving Day Parade**
Near Mr Leonards
www.metropolisthanksgivingparade.met
This Thursday spectacle starts at Mr Leonards, the acclaimed department store on Seventh Avenue, then makes a slow loop through the city's streets before ending at the store's alternate entrance on Byers Street.

early Dec **Holiday Tree Lighting Ceremony**
LexCorp Plaza
www.metropolisholidaytree.met
Due to post-attack reconstruction, this century-old tradition has been relocated to LexCorp Plaza. Ice skating, warming stations and mugs of hot cider and cocoa make this space festive throughout the holiday season.

31 Dec **New Year's Eve Celebrations**
Metro Square
www.newyearsevemetropolis.met
A three-story hologram counts down the seconds until midnight in Metro Square, the most popular destination in Metropolis for ringing in the New Year. It gets very crowded, so arrive by 4pm to reserve a spot. Bands and entertainers perform all night.

1 Jan **New Year's Day Fun Run**
Metropolis Park
www.newyearsmetropolis5k.met
Thousands of Metropolis citizens get their New Year's resolutions off to a good start, shaking off any holiday lethargy in this brisk five-kilometre (three-mile) run, which begins at 6am.

Metro Square on New Year's Eve

Remembering the attack

A tragedy and its aftermath.

An alien transmission, broadcast across the globe, soon led to the activation and destruction of an unimaginably powerful superweapon. No one could have predicted that events would unfold where they did, in the middle of downtown Metropolis.

It is a testament to the spirit of the people of this city that the question of 'why here?' didn't get in the way of decisive action. Immediately, rescue crews and volunteers descended on Metropolis to find survivors and remove the bodies of the fallen. But clearing the rubble was going to take months, and a two-part plan emerged for how a space marked by tragedy could be reappropriated with respect. The epicenter of the shockwave – a healed scar at the heart of the city – would remain undeveloped as a memorial and a reminder. Everything else would be built anew to prove that grief would not paralyze Metropolis.

Heroes Park p34

Heroes Park

Beautiful lawns and trees have bloomed anew on the former Centennial Park, the site of 2013's Kryptonian attack on the city. After the tragedy, the Park was renamed Heroes Park, a place of reverence and contemplation where visitors are encouraged to keep their voices low, so as not to disturb mourners. Fallen heroes and brave survivors are both honored here, and the Superman statue is a central (and controversial) landmark.

At the Memorial Booth beneath the Heroes Park Monorail station, visitors can sign out free audio players and headphones, which provide a narrative accompaniment for self-guided tours that explain the events that took place on the site. The wreck of an otherworldly craft still rests in the park, but is off-limits to the public.

New construction

LexCorp led the efforts to rebuild Metropolis to even greater heights than before. Having watched his half-completed LexCorp Tower collapse into ruins during the event, tech entrepreneur Lex Luthor broke ground on a new HQ the very next day. The construction of LexCorp Plaza – including the new LexCorp Tower, the Lexor Hotel, and a pedestrian plaza – gave thousands of local people meaningful employment and demonstrated a way forward for those struggling with incomprehensible devastation. The skyline surrounding Heroes Park is now transformed, and LexCorp Tower is the tallest building in Metropolis.

Metropolis

Daily Planet Building

Sights & Museums

Throughout its history Metropolis has famously looked towards the future. The maglev monorails that crisscross the city are one of the most visible signs of the march of human progress, and every warehouse seems to harbor a tech incubator or a maker's workshop. At its core, Metropolis is optimistic, and it is this attitude that has allowed the city to bounce back so strongly from the recent tragedy. The grass of Heroes Park has healed the urban scars left by the Kryptonian attack, and a flurry of new construction – crowned by the gleaming spire of **LexCorp Tower** – is reshaping downtown. The most memorable icons of the city still stand proudly, including **Hammersmith Tower** and the **Daily Planet Building**, while Metropolis' numerous museums and its **Avenue of Tomorrow** tech showcase are evidence that intelligence can win out over violence.

Avenue of Tomorrow
Avenue of Tomorrow, between Fifth Street & 22nd Street (1-637 555 0180). Monorail B, C, D to Avenue of Tomorrow Station. **Map** p28 A3 ❶

Midtown is bisected by this high-tech thoroughfare, which has been the site of epochal events in the history of human progress. It was the first street illuminated by electric light, the first with maglev monorail tracks, and the first with an electric car recharging station. Amble down the wide, pedestrian-friendly sidewalks and browse storefronts promoting products from Wayne Enterprises, Kord Industries and – of course – LexCorp. At the intersection of Wardenclyffe Street and the Avenue of Tomorrow, you'll find Metro Square (p33).

City Hall
2100 Second Avenue, at Potsdam Street (1-632 555 0159, www. metropoliscityhall.met). Monorail B, C, D, E to Second Avenue Station.

Closed to the public, but tours available by appointment. **Map** p28 A3 **②**
The mayor and city council of Metropolis conduct their business inside this Beaux-Arts architectural masterpiece built in 1849. Tours (free) are available, though high-school field trips take up most of the available slots.

Daily Planet Building

330 Sixth Street, at Concord Lane (1-632 555 0108, www.dailyplanet.met). Monorail B, C, D, F to Heroes Park Station. **Open** *Tours* 10am, noon, 2pm daily. **Admission** *Tours* $15; $10 reductions. **Map** p28 C2 **③**
Metropolis' leading newspaper, the *Daily Planet* has chronicled events in the city and across the globe since 1871. In 1952, the *Planet* moved its editorial offices into this clean-lined modernist skyscraper, ousting the previous occupant the *Daily Star* in a muscle-flexing war between media moguls. In the end, *Planet* co-owner Morgan Edge carried the day, and most now consider the *Planet* the nation's paper of record. In recent years, the *Planet* has made a smooth transition into digital news aggregation and online reporting. The bronze planet sphere in the lobby is an oft-photographed symbol of the city.

Geschäft-Krieg Building

500 Wardendyffe Street, at Avenue of Tomorrow. Monorail B, C, D, E to Metro Square Station. Closed to the public. **Map** p28 A4 **④**
Perhaps no building exemplifies Metropolis' aesthetic as well as the headquarters of Geschäft-Krieg, the defense contractor occupying one of the city's most beautiful high-rises. The interior is closed to the public, but architecture connoisseurs are drawn to the retro-futurist façade – an art deco vision of the future.

Glenmorgan Square

Raum Avenue & Green Street (1-632 555 0160, www.glenmorgansquare.met).

Avenue of Tomorrow

METROPOLIS

Lexcorp Tower

Monorail B, C, D to Financial Circle Station. **Open** 24hrs daily. **Admission** free.

Bumping up against the waterfront on the Lower East Side, Glenmorgan Square is a concrete park surrounded by high-rise banking HQs, just blocks from Metropolis University. Named after the wealthy Glenmorgan family of investment traders, the triangular expanse fills up with food carts and hungry lunch-breakers every weekday from 11am to 2pm.

Hammersmith Tower

1800 Cleveland Street, at Second Avenue (1-632 555 01 44, www. hammersmithtower.met). Monorail B, C, D, E to Metro Square Station. Closed to the public. **Map** p28 A5 ⑤

This 1930s skyscraper boasts a handsome art deco clock face and chimes that have tolled for generations of locals. For a brief time after the Kryptonian attack, the Hammersmith

was once again the tallest building in Metropolis until it was overtaken by the new LexCorp Tower (p35).

Heroes Park

N of Sullivan Street & W of Butler Street (www.heroespark.met). Monorail B, C, D, F to Heroes Park Station. **Open** 24hrs daily. **Admission** free.

Map p29 D2 ⑥

From end to end, Heroes Park (formerly Centennial Park) covers what was once the nexus of the devastation visited upon the city during the recent tragedy. Rebuilding the toppled skyline has become an important part of the city's recovery, but the creation of Heroes Park ensured that ground zero for the gravity-wave impact would remain a quiet place of remembrance and reflection. The names of those who lost their lives on that day – and the statues of those who emerged as heroes – are on display here, with self-guided audio tours providing history and context.

Pick up a free audio player and earbuds at the Memorial Booth beneath the Heroes Park Monorail station. Still on site is the crashed spacecraft involved in the attack, but it remains out-of-bounds to visitors.

Jules Verne Extra-Terrestrial Museum

9900 Iroquois Avenue, at Olivia Street (1-637 555 0153, www.jvetm.met). Monorail H to Bakerline Terminal. **Open** 10am-8pm Mon-Sat; 10am-5pm Sun. **Admission** $12; free-$8 reductions. Dreams of the future are filtered via the lens of the past in this quirky sci-fi museum inspired by 19th-century writer Jules Verne and the steampunk-ish vibe of his acclaimed adventure novel *20,000 Leagues Under the Sea*. Get up close with movie memorabilia, or listen to a recording of Orson Welles' infamous broadcast of HG Wells' *The War of the Worlds*, which panicked listeners in 1938.

Julian Gallery

570 Waterfront Street, at Howard Court (1-637 555 0102, www.juliangallery. met). Monorail B, C, D, E to Queensland Docks Station. **Open** noon-6.30pm Mon-Sat. **Admission** $15; $10 reductions.
The centerpiece of this maritime museum is an 18th-century Spanish galleon, raised from the ocean floor by the Lemaris Foundation. Shipwreck artefacts and strange relics attributed to the lost civilization of Atlantis attract the curious.

LexCorp Tower

LexCorp Plaza, at Tilton Avenue (1-637 555 0100, www.lexcorp.met). Monorail B, C, D to Avenue of Tomorrow Station. **Open** *Visitor Center* 8am-7pm Mon-Sat. **Admission** free. **Map** p28 B3 **7**
In a city famous for its visionaries, Lex Luthor is unique in his bold plan for Metropolis' future and his generosity in helping the city get back on its feet after the attack. Construction of this building, the world HQ of LexCorp, was half-finished until its destruction in the tragedy – but Luthor announced its rebuilding the very next day. Now open for business, the Tower reaches to the heavens as a symbol of human resilience and accomplishment. The eagerly awaited Skydeck viewing platform, on the 50th floor, opens in 2016.

Metro Square

Wardendyffe Street & Avenue of Tomorrow. Monorail B, C, D, E to Metro Square Station. **Map** p28 A5 **8**
The blinking advertisements and rotating spotlight beams at this intersection are the unmistakable signs of Metro Square, one of Metropolis' most visited sites. Take a selfie at the photo-op podium, or browse the touristy knick-knacks in the souvenir shops.

Metropolis History Museum

1220 12th Street, at Longshore Avenue (1-632 555 0139, www.metropolis historymuseum.met). Monorail C, F

METROPOLIS

Metropolis History Museum p35

Metropolis Park

N of Bloomsbury Street, W of Fifth Avenue. Monorail H, K to Metropolis Park Station. Open sunrise-sunset daily. Admission free.

Take a breather from the fast pace of urban life in this public recreation area. Despite its relatively compact size, Metropolis Park makes good use of its acreage with forested switchback trails and spaces set aside for picnicking and intramural sports. Canoeing and kayaking are permitted in the park's reservoir. The tree planting is something special too, with white and pink clouds of cherry blossom in spring, and breathtaking fall colours.

Metropolis Science Exploratorium

321 Cyrus Street, at Vale Street (1-637 555 01 28, www.metscienceexploratorium.met). Monorail B to Queensland Park Terminal. Open 8.30am-8pm Mon-Sat; 10am-8pm Sun. Admission $16; $8-$12 reductions.

Take the bridge to Queensland Park and spend a day in this marvellous science museum, where the city's legacy of innovation is celebrated through interactive exhibits and live demonstrations. Don't miss the walk-through re-creations of Metropolis during the colonial era, the industrial revolution, and the 1960s space race. Visitors can also see the experimental 'space plane' *Constitution* up close. While the museum builds a permanent home for the craft, the exhibition plays host to monthly fundraising cocktail parties.

Metropolis Museum of Art

220 Second Street, at Fifth Avenue (1-632 555 01 79, www.metropolismoa.met). Monorail B, C, D, E to Fashion District Station. Open 10am-7.30pm Mon-Sat. Admission $18; free-$14 reductions.

Works of the Old Masters are proudly represented in the MMA, which has world-class collections covering the Renaissance as well as Impressionism, Fauvism, Cubism and art deco. It also has one of the world's largest collections of Tamara de Lempicka's works. The gift shop is a trove of unusual souvenirs and art books.

Built on the site of historic Fort Hob, this popular, child-friendly attraction on the waterfront offers an interactive journey through Metropolis' role in shaping American history. Highlights include a miniature model of the city built in 1949 and a 3D holographic version of the same, recently gifted to the museum by LexCorp.

to Hob's Bay Station. Open 9.30am-8pm Mon-Sat. Admission $20; $12-$15 reductions. Map p29 E3 **9**

Chez Joey's p38

Eating & Drinking

They say the sun always shines in Metropolis, and the city's wealth of outdoor cafés seems to support the claim. In warm weather, even the four-star restaurants will offer sidewalk seating, the perfect spot for people-watching – or for catching a telltale streak of blue and red zipping across the sky at supersonic speed. Chefs, maître d's, and wait staff are famously accommodating and friendly, leaving no doubt that the city has made a near-total recovery from the recent tragedy. The busy environs of the rebuilt Midtown offer quick-service diners, where you might bump elbows with media moguls on their lunch break. Upscale steakhouses dominate the West River waterfront, where the pricier menus come with a breathtaking view of the bay and the distant lights of Gotham City. Venture to Hob's Bay for a more rough-around-the-edges experience, to knock back a brew at your new favorite corner bar.

Ace O'Clubs

11 Turf Street, between Bay Avenue & Longshore Avenue (1-632 555 0132). Monorail C, F to Hob's Bay Station. **Open** 4pm-4am Mon-Sat. **Bar** **Map** p29 E2 ①

It's not much to look at, but few taverns have the authentic cachet of the Ace. Owned by ex-prize fighter Bibbo Bibowski – who often tends bar and chats with patrons – the Ace has been called a lucky charm by the Hob's Bay dockworkers who patronize it. Because Bibbo bought the bar with lottery winnings, legend says that those who rub its doorknob will find good fortune. It's a frequent stop for tourists who brave 'Suicide Slum', and its annual St Patrick's Day bash is unforgettable.

Alewife

3501 Second Avenue, at Cornelius Street (1-632 555 0113, www.alewifedining. med). Monorail B, C, D, E to Queensland Docks Station. **Open** 11am-10pm daily. $$$ Seafood

One of the best-kept secrets of the Queensland Docks, the Alewife is where commercial fishermen head to enjoy a good fish dinner. Crab cakes and lobster rolls go down well with a frosted Koul-Brau lager. Try the Blue Point oysters on the half-shell, or a bubbling bouillabaisse of mackerel, cod, and mussels.

Bessolo Bistro

22 Waterfront Street (1-637 555 0138, www.bessolobistro.met). Monorail B, C, D, E to Queensland Docks Station. **Open** 10am-midnight Mon-Thur, Sun; 10am-1am Fri, Sat. **$$. American**
With romantic lighting and bay windows providing spectacular views of the Atlantic, Bessolo Bistro makes the most of its location near the tip of New Troy island. Prices are surprisingly reasonable in this longtime neighborhood hangout, which sees the blue-collar lunch-break crowd rub elbows with Metropolis celebrities. Tuck into hearty dishes including blue cheese meatloaf and spiced apple pancakes. The back room is lined with signed photos and memorabilia spanning decades of Metropolis history.

Big Belly Burger

Multiple locations (1-637 555 0164, www.bigbellymetropolis.met). **Open** 6am-11pm daily. **$. Burgers**
This chain started on the West Coast, but when franchises started popping up along the Atlantic, both Metropolis and Gotham City claimed the thick-cut, paper-wrapped burgers as their own. Metropolis Big Belly locations have a custom menu that includes meat patties seasoned with minced olives. Parent company LexCorp sometimes tests new innovations in food science at local Big Bellys, with the 100-calorie milkshake a recent smash hit.

Carlini's

110 Fifth Street, between Second Avenue & Bessolo Boulevard (1-632 555 0177, www.carlinis.met). Monorail B, C, D, E to Fifth Street Station. **Open** 5pm-1am Mon-Sat. **$$$. Italian**
Map p28 A1 ⓫
One of the city's highest-rated Italian *ristorantes*, Carlini's serves familiar old-country favorites alongside zesty dishes such as egg-vinegar ravioli and 23 varieties of stuffed sausages. An adjoining bakery offers take-out delights – do try the cannoli.

Carrasco's

340 Barter Street, at Patton Street & Harnden Way (1-635 555 0177, www.carrascos.met). Monorail H, I, K to Thornton Station. **Open** 11am-9pm Mon-Sat. **$$. Chilean**
The first thing you'll notice at Carrasco's is the smell of corn *humitas*. Sweet or savory, they're worthy appetizers to the flaky, flawless empanadas (there are variations, but stick with the classic: beef, raisins, egg and olives) and the *pastel de chodo*. Enjoy a glass of red from the deep-bench wine list, but don't forget the cocktails – the *pisco* menu is nearly as long. In a city always surging toward tomorrow, Carrasco's never forgets its roots.

Chaney's

110 Bay Avenue, between Sullivan Street & Tilton Avenue (1-637 555 0120, www.chaneys restaurant.met). Monorail C, F to Hob's Bay Station. **Open** 2pm-midnight Mon-Sat. **$$$. Fusion**
Map p29 E2 ⓬
This trendy addition to Hob's Bay serves up fusion dishes – masala macaroni and mango chicken poppadoms among them – under the direction of entrepreneurial chef Carmen Chaney. Unlike the food, the decor is all pared-down minimalism.

Chez Joey's

3321 Sterling Street, at Sixth Avenue (1-632 555 0103, www.chezjoeys.met). Monorail B, D, F to Wardendyffe Station. **Open** 3pm- midnight Mon-Sat; noon-7pm Sun. **$$$$. American**
Map p28 C4 ⓭

always crowded.

Situated next to the *Daily Planet* building, Dooley's has been an institution for generations of reporters, editors, and other ink slingers. Fare tends toward burgers, dogs, and bowls of chili, but the real attractions are the framed *Daily Planet* front pages that cover a century's worth of memorable headlines. The bar offers 25 beers on tap and is

Dooley's Pub
$$$ Diner/Bar Map p28 C1 ❶⁴
320 Fifth Street, at Concord Lane (1-632 555 0195, www.dooleys.met). Monorail B, C, D, E to Fashion District Station. **Open** *10am–1am Mon-Sat.*

Chez Joey's is a prized destination for anniversary diners, Valentine's, and the toasting of business partnerships. It's upscale, but not austere, with a long bar, a more formal seating area, and bold industrial lighting. The plates are small, but rich: New American with Japanese touches, emphasizing umami on dishes such as the unbeatable beef tartare and the can't-miss pumpkin toast with miso. For the main course, order the wood-scented cod, or the Wagyu cheese burger. If you can, score a table by the kitchen to watch the magic happen.

Dynasty
620 12th Avenue, at Sharpe Street (1-632 555 0186, www.dynasty restaurant.met). Monorail B, D, E, K to Chinatown Station. **Open** *11am–11pm Mon-Sat, 10am–9pm Sun.* $$$$
Pan-Asian **Map p29 E5** ❶⁵

Anchoring the south-west corner of Chinatown, the sprawling Dynasty contains five kitchens and promotes an Asian-fusion menu that leans on Chinese, Vietnamese, Thai, Japanese and Korean influences. A popular destination for first-time visitors to Chinatown, Dynasty fills up quickly on weekends. Reservations are not taken.

Evans Pretzel Factory
2100 14th Street, between Seventh Avenue & Concord Lane (1-632 555 0155, www.evanspretzel.met). Monorail B, C, E to Apricot Station. **Open** *6am–11pm Mon-Sat, 8am–7pm Sun.* $, **Snacks** **Map p28 C3** ❶⁶

The vast, brick-walled expanse of Evans isn't just for show – that's an actual, working pretzel factory behind its welcoming storefront. The unmistakeable buttery aroma that wafts from the windows has been ensnaring locals for over 75 years. The neon letters of the iconic Evans sign – normally

Chaney's

Eating & Drinking

is always in flux; chef Matthew Taggio uses molecular tricks on seasonal ingredients for challenging, surprising results. Notables such as Contessa Erica Del Portenza (a regular) can get a table any time they like, but take mortals have to book months in advance.

Mo's Café

91 Bay Avenue, between Sullivan Street & Tilton Avenue (1-632 555 0191, www.moscafe.net). Monorail C, F to Hob's Bay Station. **Open** 5am-9pm daily. **$$ Café Map** p29 E2

Looking for a wake-up call in a cup? Try Mo's signature cold coffee with mulling spices. Offset the caffeine jitters with a game-changing (read: massive) ham, egg and aioli breakfast sandwich, the 'Hob's Hammin''. The café, which survived a near-shutdown in the 1970s, is now so popular among Hob's Bay residents that a 30- to 45-minute wait for weekend seating is normal.

Uri's Family Restaurant

8890 Mundell Street, at Hillis Street (1-637 555 0144, www.uris.net). Monorail C, F to Silas Station. **Open** 7am-9pm daily. **$$ Diner**

LexCorp recently acquired the Uri's chain and announced plans to spread the franchise globally. The original Uri's on Mundell contains no hint of such grand ambitions, with its humble diner counter and narrowly packed tables. But order the corned beef bagel sandwich or the grilled fish sliders and you'll know why locals have lunched at this spot for over 75 years.

electric blue – glow red whenever the 'pretzel benders' have worked up a fresh batch for customers. Weekend factory tours are available.

Karl's Pump & Brew

672 Atkinson Avenue, at Van Lew Street & Silas Street (1-637 555 0148, www.karlspumpandbrew.met). Monorail H, I to Silas Station. **Open** 11am-1pm Mon-Sat; 11am-7pm Sun. **$$ Barbecue**

This former auto repair shop takes its gimmick to the limit, ushering diners into themed seating areas such as Muscle Car Mile or the Detroit Room. Some tables sit directly beneath classic cars mounted on maintenance lifts. Karl's has live music every Friday and Saturday night.

Koul-Brau Breweries

432 14th Street, at 11th Avenue (1-635 555 0121, www.koulbrau.met). Monorail H, I, K to Laverty Station. **Open** 11am-2am Mon-Sat; 11am-5pm Sun. **Brewpub Map** p29 D3

Franchised Koul-Brau brewpubs have started popping up all over the East Coast, but Metropolis is home to the original. Founded on this spot following the repeal of Prohibition, Koul-Brau still bottles its signature lager but is better known today for its stouts, red ales, and gluten-free brews. Despite howls from purists, the company's recent acquisition by LexCorp hasn't watered down its product in the least. Stop by for a pint, and a pizza – from the new wood-fired brick oven.

LeMarvin Bistro

998 Tobie Street, at Kingsley Street (1-637 555 0172, www.lemarvinbistro.met). Monorail C, D, F to Park Ridge Station. **Open** 4pm-midnight Mon-Sat; 1-10pm Sun. **$$$$ Eclectic**

The interior is a just a monochromatic lab, but the lighting is perfect, the atmosphere stunning, the cocktails excellent – and that's before the food's even arrived. It's hard to recommend dishes at LeMarvin's because the menu

Ace O'Clubs p37

Shopping

Metropolis rivals Tokyo as a global capital for consumer electronics, and the city's long-standing reputation as a tech hub has recently received a quantum boost thanks to LexCorp's investment in 'innovation campuses'. The LexCorp store on Tesla Avenue proudly displays advances that are years away from hitting the American heartland – you can often spot a local by the unmistakable beeping rectangle tucked discreetly into a shirt pocket. And no self-respecting tourist returns home without a futuristic Metropolis gizmo to show off to their friends and relatives.

That forward-thinking attitude extends to clothing styles too, with a Fashion District that has received an injection of fresh energy from designers inspired by deco lines and bright colors. Few visitors can leave the city without indulging in souvenir shopping, and Metropolis mementos can be surprisingly

Blaze Comics

1935 Cleveland Street, at Fourth Avenue (1-632 555 0154, www.blazecomics.net). Monorail B, C, D, E to Metro Square Station. **Open** 9am-9pm Mon-Sat; 9am-4pm Sun. **Map** p28 B3 ⑲

Metropolis's oldest comic-book shop has multiple locations throughout the city and the suburbs, but this two-level downtown location – directly beneath the editorial offices of Blaze Publishing – started it all. Snap up a Commander Courage notebook or totebag, or get caught up in the adventures of the Astro Teens with bargain-priced comics. Today, in light of the emergence

and bright colors. Few visitors can advanced, with snow-globe skylines incorporating nano-lighting that responds to the time of day and the weather. The Kryptonian attack has given rise to a cottage industry of somber – and occasionally tacky – remembrances, but if you want a Superman keepsake you'll have to check in with the bootleggers.

Blaze Comics

of Metropolis' real-life superhuman protector, the fantastical tales of Blaze Comics seem downright prescient.

Digby & Sons

432 Haskell Street, at Eighth Street (1-632 555 0102, www.digbyandsons. met). Monorail B, C, D, E to Fashion District Station. **Open** 10am-9pm Mon-Sat; 10am-5pm Sun. **Map** p28 B2 ㉙

The longtime rival of Schwartzenoff (p44) for wallet share among customers visiting the Jewelry District, Digby & Sons opened in 1909 inside a Greek-columned edifice originally built for a bank. In Metropolis, a velvet-lined box from Digby & Sons is a traditional accompaniment for marriage proposals and anniversary celebrations.

Empire Pier

3350 Hob's River Drive, at 12th Street (1-632 555 0107, www.empirepier.met). Monorail C, F to Hob's Bay Station. **Open** 8am-midnight Mon-Sat; 9am-9pm Sun. **Map** p29 F3 ㉑

This tourist-friendly destination drew the ire of locals when it opened for business in 1996, but Empire Pier is now one of the most visible signs of a city that's open for business after the recent attack. Chain restaurants and carnival rides share space with an enclosed mini-mall, where shoppers can find nautically themed trinkets alongside a children's playplace and a 20-screen movieplex.

Mary Alice's Consignment Shop

4332 Withington Boulevard, between Doolittle Street & Bloomsbury Street (1-632 555 0141, www.maryalice consignment.met). Monorail I, K to Doolittle Station. **Open** 8am-9pm Mon-Sat; 9am-4pm Sun.

Far removed from the Fashion District is this darling of deal-chasing local fashionistas. Overruns, irregular items and last season's designs are offered here at discounts ranging from 30% to a staggering 90% off retail prices.

Arrive early for the best deals – by 11am, the 'daily discount' tables have been thoroughly picked over.

Metro Souvenirs

110 Sixth Street, at Second Avenue (1-637 555 0176, www.metro souvenirs.met). Monorail B, C, D, E to Second Avenue Station. **Open** 8am-10pm daily. **Map** p28 A2 ㉒

Most visitors leave Metropolis laden with an armload of keepsakes for friends and family. At Metro Souvenirs, you can wrap up your shopping list in one go, thanks to a three-level gallery that spans the price range from novelty keychains and discount-rack T-shirts on the ground floor, to designer scarves and limited-run art prints at the top of the building.

Mr Leonards

1700 Seventh Avenue, at Fifth Street (1-637 555 0198, www.mrleonards.met). Monorail B, C, D, E to Fashion District Station. **Open** 8am-10pm Mon-Sat; 9am-5pm Sun. **Map** p28 C1 ㉓

The Fashion District would hardly be recognizable without the rock-solid presence of Mr Leonards, the classic department store whose breadth of merchandise revolutionized urban shopping when it opened in 1915. Online retailers may have taken a bite out of the store's profits in recent years, but the store is still a must-see destination for visitors. During the holiday season, Santa's Village takes up most of the third floor, while elaborate window displays entice sidewalk gawkers. Start at Mr Leonards and head off in any direction – you'll find endless shopping options in the surrounding blocks, which have been unofficially designated as the shoe district, the garment district, and the fur district.

Schott's Toys

12 South Simon Street (1-637 555 0163, www.schottstoys.met). Monorail C, F to Hob's Bay Station. **Open** 10am-8pm Mon-Sat; 9am-4pm Sun. **Map** p29 E1 ㉔

METROPOLIS

METROPOLIS

Digby & Sons p43

This recent addition to Hob's Bay has earned raves for its handcrafted and vintage playthings. Porcelain dolls, tin soldiers and other toys that wouldn't have been out of place a century ago are given a modern twist with voice-recognition software and reactive intelligence that adapts to the environment. Prices are high, but you can test out the demo models for free.

Schwartzenoff

601 Byers Street, at Seventh Street (1-632 555 0104, www.schwartzenoff.met). Monorail B, C, D, E to Fashion District Station. Open 10am-9pm Mon-Sat; 10am-3pm Sun. Map p28 C2

The blocks between Schwartzenoff and its rival Digby & Sons (p43) comprise the Jewelry District, a world-class marketplace of gemstones and precious-metal settings. Schwartzenoff opened in 1910 – just one year after its chief competitor – and helped set the tone for the district's air of slow-paced formality. Many sales attendants have worked for the store for 20 years or more; some have worn the starched gray uniform for over a half-century.

Superman merchandisers at Heroes Park

Heroes Park, Monorail B, C, D, F to Heroes Park Station

Seemingly every visitor to Metropolis wants to know more about the city's so-called 'Superman', but the man himself has so far remained a mystery. There's no officially licensed Superman swag – at least, not yet – but that hasn't stopped opportunists from manufacturing their own merch and hawking it on street corners. In Heroes Park (p34), you'll find a dizzying selection of items, from oil paintings to belt buckles to light-up spinning tops, all emblazoned with the familiar 'S' shield.

Company matters

LexCorp: past, present and future.

Though it bears the same name, the corporation headed by Alexander Joseph Luthor Jr is nearly unrecognizable compared to the petrochemical and heavy machinery behemoth founded by his father. Both incarnations of the company have profoundly shaped Metropolis, but it is the quantum-leap innovations coming from the current 'next-tech' giant that are setting the course for the city of tomorrow.

The LexCorp legacy

Seeking freedom from authoritarianism, Alexander Luthor Sr emigrated to the United States from East Germany. In Metropolis, he discovered an open attitude toward industrial development, leading to rapid progress and billion-dollar profits. Whole sections of the Financial District and Midtown wear their familiar skylines thanks to urban infrastructure investments laid down by the LexCorp of old.

Times of transition

Alexander Luthor Sr died unexpectedly in 2000. To critics, his college-aged son seemed like a poor fit for a moneyed industrial empire – and to everyone's surprise, Lex Luthor Jr agreed. The genius wunderkind set to work reimagining his father's creation, transforming LexCorp into a leading force in the fields of science and technology. The new LexCorp was perfectly positioned to take advantage of revolutions in genome sequencing, nano-robotics and personal connectivity. By the age of 31, Lex Luthor was the youngest-ever

Fortune Businessperson of the Year, and LexCorp had rocketed to the rank of the second-largest tech company in the world, behind Gotham City's Wayne Enterprises.

Building a future

The tragic events of 2013 only accelerated Lex Luthor's plans for Metropolis. It was LexCorp that spearheaded the city's reconstruction efforts, and the all-new LexCorp Tower took shape in less than 18 months. This combination of breathtaking ambition and tangible progress proved to the world that Metropolis was open for business, attracting a flurry of international investment and goodwill.

Unlike many executives, Lex Luthor is frequently spotted in public, and not just at five-star restaurants. This gregarious whiz kid holds season tickets for the Metropolis Mammoths and mingles daily with the lunchtime crowds that fill LexCorp Plaza.

Elsewhere, LexCorp's philanthropic efforts have benefited low-income housing in Hob's Bay and museums and libraries in Midtown. Visionary futurism is the order of the day at LexCorp's 'inspiration stations,' where employees eat gourmet lunches and scale climbing walls in between intense sessions of computer coding. To some, LexCorp's recent expansion into military defense stands to benefit Metropolis even more by introducing methods of stopping the next Kryptonian-style attack before it can begin.

METROPOLIS

Metropolitan Club p48

Nightlife

METROPOLIS

In the weeks following the Kryptonian attack, Metropolis' nightlife shut down as construction workers and community volunteers turned their attention to the immediate crisis. The scene rebounded, however, as residents sought to shed their stresses at taverns and late-night clubs. There are plenty of places to get a taste of this communal energy, particularly in a city famous for its music scene, where seemingly every bar has an open microphone.

Nova and similar velvet-rope dance clubs helped shape the city's glitzy pop-culture history. Catch headliner acts at larger venues such as **Shuster Arena** (p53) or **Siegel Music Hall**, or get close to the stage in the intimate performance spaces scattered throughout Hob's Bay and along the periphery of the Met U campus. You can party next to the Monorail tracks at the stroke of midnight and judge a poetry slam in the wee hours approaching daybreak. And every month, new venues pop up across the city in a flurry of creative entrepreneurship.

Border Room
8892 MacGowan Street, at Gatling Street (1 637 555 0135, www.border room.met). Monorail B, F to Gatling Street Station. **Open** 3pm-1am Tue-Sat; 3-11pm Sun.
Metropolis is a healthy city, and there aren't many places left that proudly indulge in old-school vices. The Border Room is one of the last holdouts, providing a fashionable take on the classic lounge atmosphere, with imported liquors, designer tobaccos and downtempo musical accompaniment creating a decidedly relaxed atmosphere.

El Ciento
1076 15th Street, at 12th Avenue (1-637 555 0157, www.elciento.met). Monorail B, D, E, K to Chinatown Station. **Open** 5pm-1am Mon-Sat. **Map** p29 E4 ㉕

El Ciento's central gimmick is a bar carved entirely from meteor rock. Expect high-priced table service with hundreds of imported bottles to choose from, served amid old-fashioned decor. Electronica is the music of choice.

Joy Lounge

8 South Simon Street, at Washington Boulevard (1-637 555 0183, www. joylounge.met). Monorail C, F to Hob's Bay Station. **Open** 4pm-1am Mon-Sat. **Map** p29 E1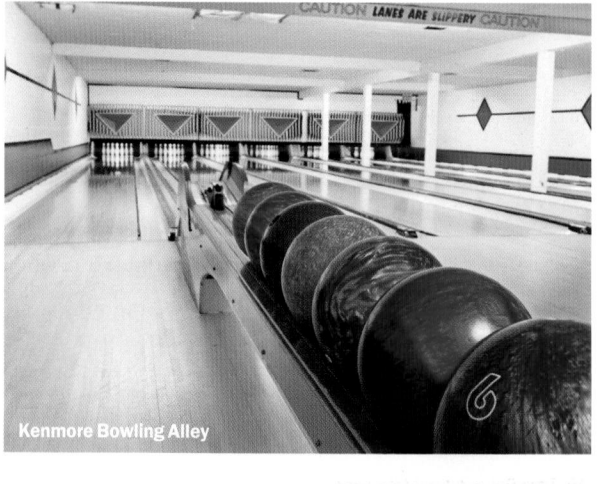

The Joy Lounge sprouted inside a former dressmaking factory, helping to transform the south-west corner of so-called Suicide Slum into a vibrant bohemian enclave. Expect poetry readings, jam sessions and open-mic confessionals, with mint tea and sesame wafers on the menu in place of alcohol and processed sugary sweets.

Kenmore Bowling Alley

8931 Iroquois Avenue, between Hall Street & Talley Street (1-632 555 0148, www.kenmorebowling.met). Monorail H to Bakerline Terminal. **Open** 11am-midnight Mon-Sat; 11am-7pm Sun.

This 1960s era bowling alley located in the suburb of Bakerline has received a hipster makeover to reflect the area's growing style-conscious demographic. Funk Night, Neon Night, Throwback Night, and other themed promotions bring in devotees of ironic kitsch to bowl a frame and polish off a pitcher of cheap brew.

Longshore Ballroom

863 Longshore Avenue, at Brady Avenue (1-632 555 0192, www.longshore ballroom.met). Monorail B, D, E, K to Chinatown Station. **Open** 7pm-1am Wed-Sat. **Map** p29 E4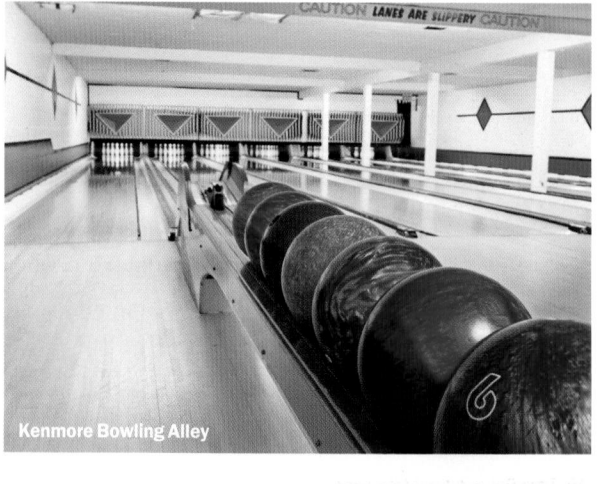

The thriving indie scene at Metropolis University often finds its first public outlet at the Longshore Ballroom, which has long been known as the place to catch local favorites before they become national sensations, serving up three back-to-back acts on a typical weekend evening.

Lucy's Pub

34 South Simon Street, at Barber Avenue (1-632 555 0198, www.lucyspub.met). Monorail C, F to Hob's Bay Station. **Open** 11am-2am Mon-Sat. **Map** p29 F1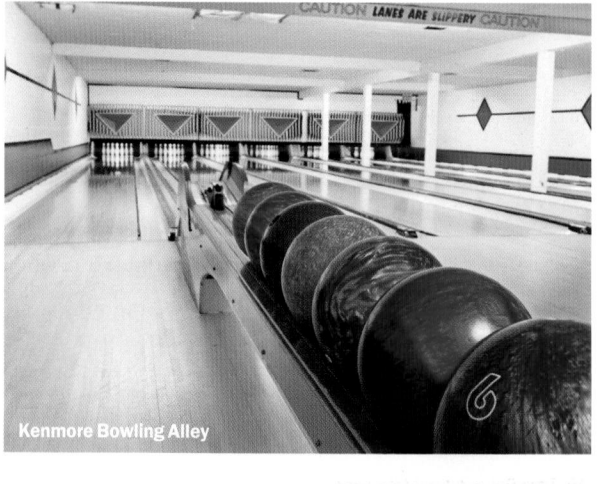

Kenmore Bowling Alley

METROPOLIS

Lucy's is dimly lit and a bit dingy, but it wears its flaws with pride. Local bands have played its stage for decades, and the echoey acoustics won't matter once you join the sweaty scrum on the packed dance floor.

Metropolitan Club

553 Fourth Street, at Avenue of Tomorrow (1-632 555 0143, www. metropolitanclub.met). Monorail B, C, D, E to Fifth Street Station. **Open** 4pm-midnight Mon-Sat; 11am-10pm Sun. **Map** p28 A1 ③⓪

Metropolis' original jazz supper club opened in 1932 and has seen a pantheon of jazz greats pass through its doors – check the black and white photographs on the walls. Headliners take the stage on Friday and Saturday nights, while the Met's house band – composed of veteran studio musicians – usually performs on weeknights.

Nova

610 Reddick Street, at 22nd Street (1-637 555 0156, www.novametropolis.met). Monorail H, K to Metropolis Park Station. **Open** 8pm-3am Mon-Sat. **Map** p28 A5 ③①

The legendary Nova has been shaping the disco and new wave scenes in Metropolis since 1975. The spot is beloved by the city's clubbing community. Today, it's as popular as ever, as evidenced by lines that stretch down the block and a door guarded by a blockade of stern-faced bouncers. The club features a monthly mash-up party with guest DJs that's worth the small cover charge. A second venue, Supernova (p49), opened in 2011.

Pit

62 Bay Avenue, at Fifth Street (1-637 555 0165, www.thepit.met). Monorail C, F to Hob's Bay Station. **Open** 8pm-2am Wed-Sat. **Map** p29 E2 ③②

This converted warehouse aims to bring the 'urban reclamation' aesthetic that's popular in Gotham City to the heart of Hob's Bay. At the no-frills Pit,

the music is loud, the crowd raucous and the drinks cheap.

Rail Line

4421 Washington Boulevard, at 15th Street (1-632 555 0136, www.therail line.met). Monorail B, D, E, K to Chinatown Station. **Open** 9pm-2am Mon-Sat. **Map** p29 E3 ③③

A decommissioned Monorail station empty since the 1970s has recently become one of the hottest nightspots on the East Side. Monorail trains roar past at top speed, rattling the floorboards of this tiny yet stunning club – which is already pulsing with the breakbeats of its drum 'n' bass mix. Because of its size, the Rail Line hits capacity quickly; once it does, you'll have to wait for someone to leave before you're allowed inside.

Siegel Music Hall

5442 East Dodd Street, at Patton Street (1-632 555 0112, www.siegelmusichall. met). Monorail C, F to Dodd Street Station. **Open** 4pm-1am Mon-Sat.

The biggest touring acts from home and abroad to hit Metropolis usually get booked into 75,000-capacity Shuster Arena (p53), but superstars with less grandiose aims are content to rock the rafters inside the 1,500-seat Siegel Music Hall. For just-announced additions to the schedule, it's best to check the website.

Sienna Hall

4211 Bessolo Boulevard, at Fifth Street (1-632 555 0178, www.sienna hall.met). Monorail B, C, D, E to Fifth Street Station. **Open** 7pm-1am Tue-Sat; 7pm-11pm Sun.

Metropolis' home for live comedy is best known for its stand-up acts, but Sienna Hall also fields a razor-sharp improv troupe on Wednesday and Thursday nights. Tuesday is the infamously brutal open-mic night, where participants must have thick skins if they hope to survive unscathed. Call ahead if you want to try your luck.

METROPOLIS

Rail Line

String Theory

16 O'Brien Street, at Remington Street (1-637 555 0160, www.stringtheory. met). Monorail H, I, K to Laverty Station. **Open** 7pm-2am Tue-Sat. **Map** p29 D4 ❸❹

This dance club, playing mainly mainstream pop and R&B alongside some indie rock, is a breakout hit with the Met U crowd. Alcohol-free nights are Wednesday and Thursday, when the minimum age for admittance is dropped from 21 to 18.

Supernova

590 Reddick Street, at 21st Street (1-637 555 0158, www.supernova.met). Monorail H, K to Metropolis Park Station. **Open** 8pm-3am Tue-Sat. **Map** p28 A5 ❸❺

This newish club is a spin-off of the legendary Nova (p48), and is located just one block north on Reddick. Where Nova is sprawling and loud, Supernova is a cozy and intimate affair

– meaning those who don't care about being seen with the in-crowd will find lots to love here. Thursdays are ladies' nights, with a waived cover charge and drink specials.

Utopia Casino

442 West Canary Street, at Van Lew Street (1-632 555 0105, www.utopiacasino.met). Monorail C, D, F to Silas Station. **Open** 24hrs daily.

The action never ends at the Utopia Casino, which offers gambling options suitable for novices and high-rollers in equal measure. Owner Tony Gallo has raised the quality of the Utopia's dining options and live entertainment acts, and he recently pledged a portion of his personal fortune toward the rebuilding of Metropolis. Gallo shares Lex Luthor's interest in rare meteorites and many specimens from his collection are displayed behind bulletproof glass on the casino's main floor.

METROPOLIS

THE WORLD'S GREATEST

DAILY PLANET

STORIES START HERE.

Take a tour of this iconic Metropolis landmark and you'll even receive your own personalized Daily Planet newspaper.

330 SIXTH ST, MONORAIL B, D, E TO HEROES PARK STATION

Arts & Leisure

From impressionistic watercolors to Russian ballet, the fine arts are in fine form in Metropolis. You can experience high culture in concentrated form by visiting the arts district, which spills across three West Side blocks and surrounds the venerable **Schaffenberger** gallery. Many theaters and music halls did not survive the infrastructure damage of the gravity-wave attack, and in some cases reconstruction is still years away. To fill the void, mobile theater companies such as the **Greico Theater Workshop** and **Awakenings Youth Theater** are giving voice to the city's new-found optimism, while stylish spas and other pockets of luxury provide well-earned opportunities for indulgence. And no matter the season, Metropolis sports are a hot ticket. Attending a home game at the **Monarchs'** Schwartz Field is a lifetime achievement for devoted baseball fans.

Apricot Spa

432 Logan Court, at Haskell Street (1-632 555 0156, www.apricotspa.met). Monorail C, D, E, F to Seventh Avenue Station. **Map** p28 B2 ③⑤

Aromatherapy, hot stone massage, reiki, and essential oils therapy are just some of the specialties offered at this upmarket spa, whose staff of specialists guarantee best-in-class treatment. A session at the Apricot will take at least half a day, so don't plan your other Metropolis activities until you've locked down a spa slot.

Awakenings Youth Theater

4170 East Miller Parkway, at Gatling Street (1-637 555 0166, www. awakeningsyouththeater.met). Monorail B, F to Arts District Station.

Metropolis public school students all undergo a two-week theatrical boot camp thanks to Awakenings Youth Theater and a recent arts and education grant. The principles of creativity,

Met U football's home: **Shuster Arena**

confidence, and self-expression are conveyed through high-spirited workshops. Courses in acting, writing, set building, and costuming are available for booking in single-day sessions, for children as young as five.

Broadrun Jazz Club
24 Fourth Avenue, at Fifth Street (1-632 555 0190, www.broadrunjazzclub.met). Monorail B, C, D, E to Fifth Street Station. **Map** p28 B1 ⓷⓻
The Broadrun is a 400-seat theater operated by the owners of the venerable Metropolitan Club (p48). The two venues work in sync, with the relaxed cocktail atmosphere of the Metropolitan helping to sharpen new acts until they're able to attract a crowd to the intimate concert environment of the Broadrun. Modal jazz, smooth jazz, and West Coast jazz acts are all on the bill, which is shared with lounge singers and American songbook crooners.

Greico Theater Workshop
Swinburne Hall, 561 Bloomsbury Street, between Raines Street & Ryan Street (1-632 555 0138, www.greicotheater workshop.met). Monorail B, F to Arts District Station.
Metropolis lacks the storied theatergoing tradition of Gotham City, but the Greico is determined to change that through public outreach. Amateurs are

welcome to try out for any show, many of which are written by accomplished local playwrights. Most performances are held at Swinburne Hall, but the Greico troupe is also a frequent sight at arts fairs and festivals.

Metro Palace Theater
3310 Fifth Avenue, between Remington Street & Sterling Street (1-632 555 0133, www.metropalacetheater.met). Monorail B, C, D, E to Metro Square Station. **Map** p28 B4 ⓷⓼
Throughout the 1920s and '30s, catching a movie at the Metro Palace Theater meant treating yourself to an opulent spectacle. Later, the place fell on hard times, closing its doors in the 1970s, but a LexCorp grant recently restored the celluloid temple to its former greatness. Red carpets and uniformed ushers help sell the time-warp illusion, while a fully stocked bar adds a nod to modern sophistication.

Metropolis Ballet
222 Fifth Street, between Second Avenue & Avenue of Tomorrow (1-632 555 0106, www.metropolisballet.met). Monorail B, C, D, E to Fifth Street Station. **Map** p28 A1 ⓷⓽
Classical dance in the city is the domain of the Metropolis Ballet, which stages classical works and story ballets when not hosting visiting dance companies.

METROPOLIS

Choreographer Leonid Stanislavovich, the company's artist-in-residence, has introduced experimental expressions inspired by unfocused primal energy.

Schaffenberger

558 Hillis Street, at Rawlings Street (1-632 555 0140, www.schaffenberger. met). Monorail B, F to Arts District Station.

The Schaffenberger gallery has stood since 1899, becoming the foundation of the arts district that gradually took shape around it. Created to house the paintings of Impressionist masters that had been acquired by shipping tycoon Horace Schaffenberger, today the gallery displays a permanent collection of works spanning the 18th through 20th centuries, as well as rotating exhibits of contemporary artists.

Simmons Gallery

3342 Bennett Street, at Marvin Way (1-637 555 0116, www.simmons.met). Monorail B, F to Bennett Street Station.

The largest gallery in the fine arts district, the Simmons hosts limited-run shows by leading notables, both old and new. It has traditionally been the auction house for (near) priceless pieces from private collections and estate sales, with some items selling for tens of millions. Auctions here are a buzzworthy confluence of celebrities and tech millionaires.

Sports teams
Baseball: Metropolis Monarchs

2100 North Brandle Street, at Vale Street (1-632 555 0150, www. metropolismonarchs.met). Monorail B to Queensland Park Terminal.

There's no denying that Metropolis is a baseball town. The hometown Monarchs play in the airy expanse of Queensland Park's Schwartz Field, which has been their home since before the Second World War. A $10-million facelift hasn't solved the ballpark's issues with obstructed-view seating because superstitious Monarchs fans

have refused to allow any alterations to the structural geometries of the arena, which has been home to eight World Series champion teams.

College football: Metropolis University

5500 South Campus Way (1-632 555 0172, www.metropolisuniversity.met). Monorail H, I, K to Laverty Station.

Football Saturdays at Met U draw 75,000 fans into the bleachers of Shuster Arena, and more than twice that many into the surrounding campus for tailgating and alumni tours. Don't miss the halftime show, when the marching band takes the field to perform choreographed odes to crowd-pleasing pop-culture hits.

Hockey: Metropolis Mammoths

7760 South Craighill Avenue, at Otis Avenue (1-632 555 0187, www. metropolismammoths.met). Monorail C to Oaktown Terminal.

From October to April, Metropolis can sometimes lie buried beneath an Atlantic-driven snowpack. When that happens there's no better time to head to AmerTek Arena, a modernized temple built around the love of hockey. Touchscreens in the arms of spectators' seats mean you can order food and drink that's delivered to you within minutes, while screens in the lobby and bathrooms keep guests updated on the action. The Mammoths are known for frequent goal-scoring and a punishing style of play, and team merchandise is a popular souvenir for Metropolis visitors.

Turley Gallery

641 Hillis Street, at Vincent Avenue (1-632 555 0128, www.turleygallery met). Monorail B, F to Arts District Station.

This striking showcase in the heart of the arts district favors modern masters with an emphasis on photography, mixed media, and found-object sculptures. Exhibits are aggressively modern, and many are intentionally designed to shock.

METROPOLIS

Essentials

New daily flights from Istanbul to Metropolis and Gotham City

METROPOLIS, MEET ISTANBUL

TURKISH AIRLINES | WIDEN YOUR WORLD

Lexor Hotel p58

Hotels

Visitors to Metropolis can enjoy a wide array of accommodation throughout the city to suit every taste – not to mention every price range. The **Park Metropolis Downtown** and **Metropolis Grand Hotel** are old-school icons of luxury in the Financial District, while the **Lexor Hotel** and other newcomers are emerging, many from the forest of construction cranes in the blocks surrounding Heroes Park. Budget-minded visitors may want to skip the centre entirely in favor of the low-priced hotel and motel chains located adjacent to the city's two major airports.

Accommodations listed below have been designated a price band to give you an idea of what you can expect to pay, but remember that rates can vary hugely according to the season or room category. As a general guide, you can expect to pay $500 or more per night for a double room in the **Deluxe** category, $300-$500 for **Expensive** hotels, $150-$300 for **Moderate** properties and under $150 for **Budget** lodgings. Don't forget to factor in Metropolis' 13% hotel tax.

Deluxe

Metropolis Grand Hotel
610 Tilton Avenue, at Concord Lane (1-637 555 0159, www.metropolis grandhotel.met). Monorail B, C, D to Seventh Avenue Station.

Catering to the city's wealthy and influential since 1922, the Met Grand boasts polished marble steps and stained-glass murals, as well as an insistence on old-fashioned formality from its smartly dressed staff. Don't forget to tip the doorman, the bellhop, and the concierge, and enjoy the pleasures of personalized attention (from tailored breakfasts to a bespoke 'pillow menu') in the heart of the Financial District.

ESSENTIALS

Park Metropolis Downtown

Expensive

Abbey

*237 Sherman Way, St Martin's Island
(1-632 555 0122, www.theabbey.met).
Boats depart from Queensland Docks;
take Monorail B, C, D, E to Queensland
Docks Station.*

The Abbey, located on tiny St Martin's Island, is only accessible by chartered boat – making it the perfect destination for a weekend spa getaway. Each of the 64 rooms has a hot tub that overlooks the ocean, providing an unforgettable way to wind down after a day filled with on-demand massages and blended-fruit breakfasts. The Abbey is open yearly from Memorial Day through Labor Day.

Atwater Tower

*470 Longshore Avenue, at 12th Street
(1-637 555 0133, www.atwatertower.
met). Monorail C, F to Hob's Bay Station.*

A popular addition to Hob's Bay, the rippled-glass silhouette of the Atwater Tower adds a distinctive touch to the waterfront skyline. Inside, a sprawling lobby/lounge is anchored by a roaring open-pit fireplace, where guests and visitors get raucous after hours. The Atwater follows a modern stripped-back aesthetic, including stainless-steel bedframes and plain concrete walls.

Lexor Hotel

*410 Tilton Avenue, between Fifth
Avenue & Sixth Avenue (1-637 555
0103, www.lexorhotel.met). Monorail
B, C, D to Seventh Avenue Station.*

Park Metropolis Downtown

*512 Byers Street, at Sullivan Street
(1-632 555 0145, www.parkdowntown.
met). Monorail B, C, D to Seventh Avenue
Station.*

A favorite of visiting CEOs and other dealmakers, the Park Metropolis is certainly set up for business: it has a conference center with 30 boardrooms, 50 high-speed video-calling pods, and a 600-seat auditorium. Hotel rooms are microcosms of thoughtful elegance, with walk-out porches and miniaturized bonsai gardens. The luxury penthouse on the topmost level is popular with (very wealthy) wedding parties.

Construction of the 239-room Lexor Hotel began immediately after the Kryptonian attack, on land buried beneath rubble. Work on the building – and the nearby LexCorp Tower (p35) – gave meaningful employment to thousands of local people, and inspired the city to take productive action in a time of uncertainty. Guests tend to be pleasantly surprised by the lower-than-expected rates. Recipients of the Rescuer Medal stay for free.

Moderate

Berkeley Lodge

730 Bloomsbury Street, between Yonkers Street & Tea Street (1-637 555 0123, www.berkeleylodge.met). Monorail B, F to Bennett Street Station.

The 86 rooms of the lovely Berkeley Lodge surround and look down upon its central attraction: a three-level swimming pool connected by a push-button system of locks and dams. You can travel between the first, third and fifth floors without ever getting out of the water, and enjoy poolside bar service until 11pm.

Centennial Hotel

310 Butler Street, between 11th & 12th Streets (1-632 555 0149, www.centennialhotel.met). Monorail C, F to Hob's Bay Station.

In the recent tragedy, this mid-priced hotel found itself just outside the radius of destruction – and soon became an impromptu headquarters for the city's recovery and reconstruction efforts. Throughout it all, the Centennial's selfless work in housing displaced victims earned its owners an enormous amount of local goodwill, and today its 154 rooms are booked at least a month in advance. The walls of the hotel lobby and the Centennial Café are covered with scrawled signatures and messages of hope from those who were eyewitnesses to the area's transformation.

Yellow Prawn

651 Labille Street, at West River Drive (1-637 555 0197, www.yellowprawn.met). Monorail B, D, E to West River Station.

This cozy B&B-style inn near the West River takes its name from the seafood and sushi eatery (worth a visit in its own right), located on the ground floor. Thirteen rooms are available, each one dressed up with a unique theme inspired by the beach houses of Cape Cod – think striped fabrics, faded wood and lots of fresh flowers. If you're planning on staying a week or more, ask about the special deals.

Budget

Bloom

880 Tracey Lane, between Lafayette Street & Ada Street (1-637 555 0169, www.bloommetropolis.met). Monorail H, I to Racine Station.

This hip motel in Park Ridge opened in 2010, but you'd swear it's actually a time-travel transplant straight out of 1969's Haight-Ashbury. Flower-power pop art and deep-pile carpeting are complemented with high-definition wallscreens and omnipresent Wi-Fi, creating a pleasing meld of the stylish and the practical.

Metropolis Athletic Club

360 33rd Street, at Bradbury Street (1-632 555 0117, www.metropolisathleticclub.met). Monorail B, C, D, E to Queensland Docks Station.

The MAC opened in lower Metropolis after World War I, providing young men with gymnasiums, showers and rooms available by the week. The modern MAC welcomes everyone, offering small but inexpensive rooms that provide a hostel-like environment and are appreciated by university crowds and foreign backpackers. Weight rooms, basketball and racquetball courts and an Olympic-sized swimming pool can be used by guests and card-carrying MAC members.

ESSENTIALS

Getting Around

Arriving & leaving

By air

Metropolis International Airport

*1-637 555 0173,
www.metropolisinternational.met.*
Metropolis' famed Monorail network sadly doesn't yet extend out as far as its airports. The cheapest transport option is the MetropolisMove shuttle service ($7, www.metropolismove. met). Buses (1-637 555 0195, www.metrotransport.met, one way $20, round trip $35) also make numerous stops within the city itself, including Hob's Bay, Midtown and the University; these run every 20 minutes (5am-10pm) and once an hour during the night. A taxi usually charges a flat fare of $60 plus bridge tolls ($5) and tip (15%). Turkish Airlines business class passengers get a free limo service – book at their new CIP lounge.

Berkowitz Airport

*1-637 555 0144,
www.berkowitzairport.met.*
From Berkowitz, your best bet is Gateway Transit (1-637 555 0127, www.gatewaytransit.met), a bus line that runs between Berkowitz and the smaller Metro City Airport in Bakerline to and from the major districts of Metropolis ($5, 45-60 minutes). A private car or taxi costs about $70 plus tolls and tip.

Public transport

Monorail

Metropolis's high-speed light rail is the envy of the world. Magnetic

levitation (maglev) technology dramatically reduces friction, leading to low energy expenditure and near-zero emissions. It also allows for blistering top speeds – Metropolis' Monorail trains can reach 90mph on long straightaways, but rarely reach such speeds within the city itself.

The Monorail runs 24/7 every day, including Christmas. Trains are identified through colors and letters, and all cars are prominently marked. Criminal incidents are rare, but take standard precautions when riding alone or late at night. You can pick up free route maps at many hotels, gift shops, or eateries, or download the interactive mobile app from **Metropolis Transit & Rail System** (1-632 555 0135, www.mtrs. met). Touchscreen route maps are on display at every station and are updated in real time to reflect delays.

Fares & tickets

You'll need to buy a **LineCard** to ride the Monorail system. These can be purchased online, at tourist kiosks, at hotel concierge desks and at touchscreen vendors at the stations themselves. Base fare for a single ride is $3, and one LineCard can be used by up to four people. Commuters tend to go for the unlimited 30-day LineCard ($135).

Boat

Metropolis' position on the Atlantic means that the city has plenty of experience in over-water transit. All ferries are governed by the **Metropolis Port Authority** (1-637 555 0188, www.mpa.met) and connect New Troy island with the outer boroughs, as well as Gotham

City. In late spring and summer, pods of dolphins sometimes surface to swim alongside the Metropolis ferries. Pick up the **Gotham City Passenger Ferry** ($7 one way, $15 day pass) near Hob's River at the Hob's Bay Station (Monorail lines C, F). **Metro Hovercraft** ($10 one way, $30 day pass) operates four high-speed ferries that depart from the tip of New Troy, two blocks from the Queensland Docks Station (Monorail B, C, D, E). Visit the website for complete ferry routes and schedules.

Bus

Bus travel is best reserved for trips that aren't time-sensitive – a typical bus trip can take twice as long as a comparable distance traveled in a taxi. Visit the **Metropolis Road Terminal** (1-632 555 0124, www. metropolisroadterminal.met) to start, at 4422 Terminal Courtyard (Terminal Courtyard Station on Monorail lines B, D, E). All bus lines can be booked here, including those connecting to the outlying suburbs.

Rail

Metropolis' light rail once extended into the heart of the city, but has since been supplanted by the Monorail network. The rail lines run through the outer boroughs and connect to the Monorail at numerous transfer stations, and to national passenger rail lines at the outskirts of the suburbs. Contact the **Metropolis Rail Authority** (1-632 555 0142, www.metropolis railauthority) for more information.

Taxis

Metropolis keeps a tight leash on its taxi drivers via the **Metropolis Taxi Commission** (1-632 555 0137, www.metropolistaxi.met). All of the seven licensed taxi lines are centrally dispatched and continuously monitored for passenger safety. Cab drivers in Metropolis have the lowest accident rate for their profession in the world. An illuminated roof light means the cab is available for hire.

Pricing start at $5, plus $0.50 per fifth of a mile or per minute idling, with a $1 surcharge during rush hour (4-8pm Mon-Fri). The average fare for a three-mile ride is $18. Always ask for a receipt, which contains the driver's number and meter number in case of complaints.

Driving

Driving in downtown Metropolis is generally not recommended, particularly now that numerous reconstruction projects have led to blocked streets and confusing traffic re-routes. Cars can be hired within the city, but are cheaper at the airports. Note that parking is extremely scarce unless you're willing to pay top prices.

Cycling

Metropolis offers rental bikes via its **UrbanCycle** program (www. urbancycle.met). More than 300 bike racks are located across the city, and bikes can be signed out for 6 hours ($5), 24 hours ($10) or 5 days ($25).

Walking

Walking is an excellent way to see Metropolis. Most streets have wide, well-lit sidewalks and easy-to-read signs that make navigation a breeze. Heart-rate monitors and stretching stations are common along many pedestrian paths. In downtown, many buildings are connected by enclosed walkways – a strollable network of second-story shops and eateries known as the **Metropolis Overstreet Mall**.

ESSENTIALS

Resources

Accident & emergency

In an emergency, dial **911** for an ambulance, police, or the fire department. The following hospitals have emergency rooms:

Hob's Bay Hospital *Longshore Avenue (1-637 555 0140). Monorail C, F to Hob's Bay Station.*
Metropolis General Hospital *3311 Yonkers Street (1-632 555 0120). Monorail C, F to Knott Station.*
Washington Medical Center *2400 Bennett Street (1-637 555 0132). Monorail B, F to Bennett Street Station.*

Internet

LexCorp Wi-Fi
www.lexcorp.io
To herald the launch of its secure operating system LEX/OS, LexCorp has installed Wi-Fi nodes all over the city to blanket Metropolis with free, high-speed wireless service. Visit the website to obtain login credentials and view a map of the network.
Metropolis Public Library
1-632 555 0188, www.metropolis publiclibrary.met.
All branches of the city's Public Library offer free online access and computers for public use (one hour per day).

Police

The Metropolis Police Department (MPD) has squad cars patrolling the city at all hours, particularly in the heavily trafficked areas of downtown as well as Hob's Bay. To find the nearest police precinct or for information about police services, call 1-632 555 0189 or visit www.metropolispd.met.

Safety

Metropolis has a reputation as a safe place to visit, and the helpfulness of local residents has only become more obvious during the city's rebuilding after the Kryptonian attack. Just the same, it is recommended to take standard precautions against street crime. Don't flaunt your money and valuables and stay away from poorly lit alleyways, particularly at night. The city's Superman is credited with stopping numerous muggings, but even he can't be everywhere at once.

Time

Metropolis is on Eastern Standard Time. This is five hours behind Greenwich Mean Time. Clocks are set forward one hour in early March for Daylight Saving Time (Eastern Daylight Time) and back one hour at the beginning of November. Going from east to west, Eastern Time is one hour ahead of Central Time, two hours ahead of Mountain Time and three hours ahead of Pacific Time.

Tipping

In restaurants, it is customary to tip at least 15%.

Tourist information

Official Metropolis Information Center at LexCorp Tower
110 LexCorp Plaza, at Tilton Avenue (1-637 555 0110, www.gometropolis. met). Monorail B, C, D to Avenue of Tomorrow Station. **Open** 8am-7pm daily.
Maps and a hotel booking service.

Spotting Superman

Where and how to see the elusive flying Super Hero.

He's been called the 'Man of Steel' by his fans – and other less charitable names by his detractors – but the city's astonishing new hero is usually just known as Superman. Gotham City may have had its own protector for decades, but Metropolis' strange visitor is very different from the nocturnal Batman. If you're visiting Metropolis, it's a good bet that you're hoping to spot Superman with your own eyes. The odds are against you as he's rarely seen, but that doesn't seem to deter anyone from trying.

Look up!

Superman can fly, so what might be mistaken in other cities for a bird or a plane might actually be a supersonic Super Hero. High-speed travel makes getting a clear photograph of Superman a tall order – by the time you get your phone out, he's usually long out of view. You're more likely to feel Superman than see him, through the sudden sonic booms that rattle skyscraper windows overhead. Be aware of your surroundings and keep scanning the skies. Even jaded locals will stop whatever they're doing to get a glimpse of Superman.

Read the Planet

The *Daily Planet* was the first news outlet to print detailed photos of the new hero. Since then, the *Planet* continues to lead the way in Superman-related news. Acts of Superman's heroism are frequently captured unfolding in real time via the *Planet*'s website or its streaming news app. The next morning, these same events are written up in the *Daily Planet*'s newspaper edition, now featuring extra content and expert analysis. In addition, the *Planet*'s online data hub collects the best long-form journalism on Superman and his origins, including award-winning articles by Lois Lane and speculations on Superman's alien nature by the scientists of S.T.A.R. Labs.

Visit Heroes Park

If you can't catch Superman in person, the second-best photo op is a trip to the Superman statue in Heroes Park. This popular attraction commemorates Superman's role in defending Metropolis against the gravity-wave assault that levelled entire blocks of downtown. Controversy over the statue's addition to the memorial site has only increased since its installation, triggering a heated debate over Superman's perceived culpability in causing the disaster, or in not doing more to minimize it.

Heroes Park is also the place to stock up on swag. Terry-cloth red capes, poseable plastic figures and ball caps bearing the familiar S-shaped symbol are all available from souvenir carts. None of the merchandise is authorized, but that hasn't put a dent in what is now a brisk trade.

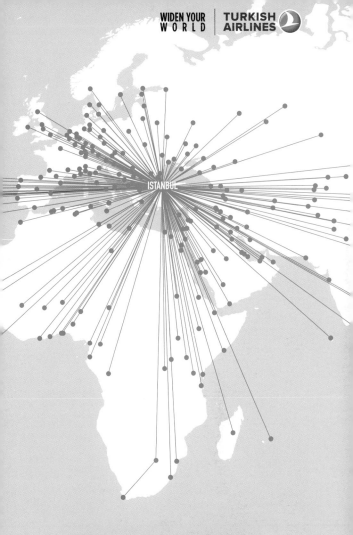

WE FLY TO MORE COUNTRIES
THAN ANY OTHER AIRLINE